9.95

22,623

940.53
W83t

THS

Wolf, Jacqueline

"Take care of Jo-
sette"

DATE DUE

"TAKE CARE OF JOSETTE"

"Take Care of Josette"

A MEMOIR IN DEFENSE OF OCCUPIED FRANCE

BY JACQUELINE WOLF

Franklin Watts
New York/ London/ Toronto/ Sydney
1981

Library of Congress Cataloging in Publication Data

Wolf, Jacqueline.
"Take care of Josette."
1. Wolf, Jacqueline.   2. Glicenstein, Josette, 1938-
3. Jews — France — Biography.
4. World War, 1939-1945 — Jews — Rescue — France.
5. Holocaust, Jewish (1939-1945) —
France — Personal narratives.
6. France — Ethnic relations.   I. Title
DS135.F9W648   940.53'15'03924   [B] 81-11411
ISBN 0-531-09861-3   AACR2

To the memory of my parents,
Paul and Cyrla Glicenstein,
deported July 13, 1942,
and of the millions of people
killed in the Holocaust.

*Many Jews in Nazi-occupied France owed their lives
to friends, neighbors, and even strangers who
risked their own lives by taking in the Jews,
harboring them throughout the war years
in cellars, attics, and secret rooms, and sharing
with them their meager food rations.
Many French citizens were imprisoned
for such actions; others were executed.*

*Because of these generous people, many Jews were
spared the horrors of the concentration camps.*

*My sister Josette and I were befriended by
these unsung heroes, about whom too little
has been said or written, and it is to them
we owe our lives. I salute them.*

FOREWORD

Why was I compelled to write about my early life? I have pondered the idea of doing this book for thirty years; yet I suspect that I have motives that are still not completely clear to me. I know that my aspirations are not for recognition of myself as I am today but for two young orphans who survived on their own the years of World War II in their native France. I also know that I have written this that I might keep alive the memory of my parents, who were killed in the prime of their lives in the most horrifying conditions because they happened to be Jewish. I know that I have written for the millions who were killed for the same reason as my parents, not by the grace of God but in an unprecedented manner dictated by a monster named Adolf Hitler.

When my beloved mother and father were taken from me, I was fourteen, an age when most children take their parents for granted; my sister Josette was only four, too young to take anyone for granted and too young to appreciate her parents—but not too young to miss their guidance and their love. And so I have written this for Josette, too.

Finally, because I am increasingly disturbed by the mounting violence that has become all too commonplace in today's world, I have written this as testament to all those selfless people who readily become their brothers' keepers.

I owe special thanks to the following people, who have generously contributed to this book: Steve Anderson and Robert Rodden who urged me to tell my story; Cara O'Donnell, who read the manuscript and made valuable suggestions; Elizabeth Hock, my editor, and Mary Ellen Casey of Franklin Watts; my husband Jonas and my son Paul, both of whom provided constant encouragement; and my daughter Michele, who patiently prepared and typed the manuscript.

Jacqueline Wolf

PART I

Where do I start? I feel I must go back to my earliest recollections. Yet, how much do I remember? I know so little about Papa and Maman.

Papa was born Paul Glicenstein in Dobra, a small town near Lodz, in Poland. My paternal grandparents were strictly religious; they observed traditional Jewish law and scorned the worldliness of others. Because of this, it was difficult for Papa and his many brothers and sisters to broaden their horizons in their parents' home; they had to attend the most rigid of parochial schools, where they could not learn much about the real world. As a result, all the children left home, one by one, and all but two emigrated to the United States. Those who stayed were my father and one of his sisters, who, along with her aunts, uncles, and cousins, was killed by the Nazis. To my knowledge, none of my father's relatives in Poland survived the war. My grandparents died of natural causes before the war began and were spared the horrors of the concentration camps.

Papa was quite tall and very slender. A handsome man, he commanded respect and admiration. His hair turned gray when he was in his early twenties, and this, along with his thick spectacles, served to intensify his remarkable blue eyes.

Papa met Cyrla Baron, my mother, during a visit to his uncle in Lodz, where the Baron family lived. People who knew my mother often remarked on her beauty. Naturally curly black hair framed her face; above round cheeks, her large oval eyes were dark and penetrating. From what I am told, I understand that it was love at first sight for both.

Maman was the third daughter in a family of five girls and one boy. Her parents were affluent storekeepers. The children were raised in the grand European manner—with private schools, tutors, and maids—by loving parents. My aunts, three of whom are still alive, recall their childhood with happiness. Grandfather and Grandmother Baron were respected in the community for their kindness and charity toward the less fortunate. Many sought my grandfather's advice on important matters. He was an educated man who spoke perfect Polish, unlike the many Jews in Poland who spoke only Yiddish.

Each of the Baron daughters was a beauty in her own right, and each received a good education. The eldest, Jeanne, died of an illness in her late teens. I am told that my grandfather died of a broken heart shortly thereafter and was followed in a matter of months by my grandmother.

Despite Papa's love for my mother, he decided that he, like his older brothers and sisters, had to leave Poland.

Long attracted to France—then considered the most prestigious country in Europe—and in love with the language, which was spoken throughout Europe by the so-called upper classes—Papa opted for Paris. Maman, by then his fiancée, promised to join him as soon as he was established.

Papa arrived in Paris in the early 1920s. He was, for a time, a jack-of-all-trades, supporting himself by sketching and working in a department store, among other jobs. Papa developed a passionate love for Paris's theaters, opera, museums, and, most of all, for the sheer beauty of the city. He used to say that one could never be lonely strolling through the streets of Paris because there was so much to be discovered. So, although his financial status at that time was often disastrous, Papa had fond memories of his humble debut in what he always called *la belle France.*

When her mother died unexpectedly, Maman decided to join my father in France, even though he was by that time hardly "established." She went to Epinal, a city in Lorraine, where she lived with a cousin for a short time until she and Papa were married. For reasons unknown to me, they decided to settle in Epinal.

In France at that time, it was worse to be a foreigner than to be Jewish. The economy was in a slump, and unemployment was high; therefore, French citizens resented any foreigners who appeared to be taking jobs that otherwise would be theirs.

Papa and Maman had no alternative but to *faire la chine* (peddle merchandise) in front of a factory in the hope of selling their wares to workers on their way to work, at lunchtime, and at closing time. The time in between they spent sitting on a park bench, in a hospitable café, or, in the winter, in the train station where it was warm.

My parents were gifted people. Papa was fluent in Polish, Russian, German, and French and could get by in several other languages. He was an accomplished, self-taught musician who played several instruments, the banjo being his favorite. He dabbled at sculpting and was quite good at sketching. An avid reader, he was even a philosopher of sorts. Above all, he loved mankind and was a friend to the underdog. Maman held a college degree in English and had worked as an English teacher in Poland. A perfectionist, she accomplished everything she set out to do, from cooking to designing clothes to sewing to decorating. But Maman's greatest interest was merchandising.

Soon after their marriage, my parents accumulated enough money to start their own business as *marchands forains*, also called *marchands ambulants* (vendors). It required quite an amount of starting capital to become a *marchand forain*, and a car was a must. (Such vendors were not unlike those who appear at farmers' markets and flea markets in this country.) My parents sold women's clothing and men's socks.

In France, as in many other European countries, one set up an *ambulant* store each day by putting up a tent and wooden tables to display merchandise.

Each town had a market day designated by the municipality. The marketplace was outside, usually in the town square. Maman and Papa spent Saturdays and Wednesdays at Epinal's market; on other days, they traveled to different towns. On Sundays they went to Gérardmer, a beautiful resort town that boasts the famous Lake Gérardmer.

[6]

My parents rose at five-thirty each morning in order to prepare for their day of selling. Getting ready for market was no easy matter, as it meant setting up their stand day after day. Papa often had to sink several tall poles in cobbled ground. The poles supported the heavy material that formed a protective awning for the folding table on which the merchandise was displayed. To this day, I can't imagine how my tall, slim Papa was able to perform this task every morning. By eight-thirty the market was open for business. The store remained open until one o'clock, when they had to fold the merchandise neatly, dismantle everything else, and return to their small panel truck for the ride home. My parents usually arrived at home between two and three o'clock in the afternoon. Even though the winters in the Vosges mountains were quite severe, neither snow nor bitter cold ever kept my parents from their exhausting work.

Eventually my parents had a thriving business. Such merchants built up a clientele, just as they would in a store. The only difference was that the low overhead of the open-air markets permitted merchants to sell their goods at much lower prices than stores could offer. Maman's talent as a businesswoman served her well in those early days.

I was born at the Hôpital Saint-Louis in Epinal. Maman had a difficult labor and delivery, with life-threatening complications, and had to remain there long after Papa took me home to the small apartment on Rue Leopoldbourg. Years later I was told that she almost lost her life bringing me into this world. Papa enlisted the aid of Maman's sister, Tante Regine, who came from Poland to live with us and take care of me. When Maman returned home several months later and regained her strength, she resumed working with Papa. It seemed only logical for Tante Regine to stay on to care for me and the household. Her stay would stretch to ten years.

I still can describe the small two-room apartment on Rue Leopoldbourg, where we lived until I was four. I remember best the curtains in my parents' bedroom, with their white crocheted design of a man and a woman in a light embrace. When I thought of those curtains in the years that followed, I imagined that the woman was Marie Antoinette and the man, Louis XVI. Other details of the apartment, of course, escape me, but I do remember that, in spite of the lack of material wealth, ours was a happy household, filled with love, laughter, and music. Papa was always playing the violin or banjo, and often the whole family would join in a sing-along.

We were still living on Rue Leopoldbourg when Papa gave me a gold chain that held a beautiful enameled medal of Moses holding the Ten Commandments, which, according to Papa, formed the basis for living. The Commandments constituted his only religious belief; they were universal in application, he said. Time and again he reminded me of this and expressed the hope that I would live by those simply stated rules.

Our financial status improved. We moved to larger and much nicer quarters at 18 Rue des Minimes. Around that time, Maman's sisters arrived: Tante Brigitte, her husband, and my cousin Ida (six months my junior), and Tante Cecile, the youngest sister, who was still single. The Baron girls, as they were called, were as striking as I had been told. Tante Brigitte, the oldest, looked somewhat like Maman, though Maman was taller. Tante Regine was blue-eyed and fair. Tante Cecile, also fair-skinned, had large green eyes and blazing red hair. They all lived nearby, on Rue des Minimes. Tante Cecile eventually married Uncle Albert, and they moved into our building; Tante Brigitte and her family lived next door. Poor Papa! It must have been a little overwhelming for him with all those women, who for some reason always gathered in our house.

My cousin Ida and I became quite close. With all those mothers around, it was never easy for us to get away with anything, but those years were happy ones. My parents were doing quite well. We had a full-time housekeeper, Germaine, a part-time seamstress, and a laundress.

I particularly liked the carefree summers and my vacation from school, when I usually joined Papa and Maman at the stand. After work on Sundays we would eat our meal at an outdoor café, then spend the afternoon by Lake Gérardmer. We swam, and often our friends joined us. It was a special, happy time for all of us.

Papa was an impeccable dresser. When I visit now with some of the older people who knew Papa well, they tell me that he was the best-dressed man in Epinal and for that reason was dubbed "the gentleman." He was just that—a gentle man. He was devoted to Maman and his family. Always a disciplinarian, Papa kept me in line with a mere look from those blue eyes. I remember being spanked only once, and I will never forget it. I stole a ten-franc silver coin—then a good deal of money—from Tante Regine and put it into a small purse. Later that day I was unable to open the clasp of the purse and asked Papa for help. He saw the coin and quickly put two and two together, because Tante Regine had complained that the same amount was missing from her purse. Usually when I misbehaved I was punished by having privileges taken away, but this time Papa tied me to a chair, rear end up, for the spanking of the century. Maman's and

Tante Regine's pleas fell on deaf ears. When Papa untied me, he held me close. I like to imagine that he had tears in his eyes, but I distinctly remember him saying, "You'll have trouble sitting down for just a week, but I hope you'll remember this forever. You'll never steal again."

Papa had an inquisitive nature. He once told me, "Don't ever be ashamed to say 'I don't know' and to ask questions. An intelligent human being learns until he dies."

No doubt Papa wanted me to have all the educational advantages he was denied as a child. He told me often that I would be the first woman lawyer in the family. This was a tall order, and of course Papa didn't realize what an impact his statement had on me. I thought I could never live up to his expectations; my schoolwork suffered considerably as a result. Papa could not accept my failure, so he hired a tutor to come to our home every day after school. Papa hoped, too, that I would follow in his footsteps with regard to music and to achieve this end hired a music teacher for me. How I hated that man! My teacher was quite an artist, as I recall, but he was also an alcoholic with bad breath. And because I was not at all musically inclined—not for the violin, the piano, or the accordion, anyway—I was not about to suffer his breath for the sake of my art. I practiced because Papa wanted me to practice, and the lessons went on until the war broke out.

I attended the Lycée d'Epinal, a private coed school, until the third grade. I was quite a tomboy, and this must have caused my parents and teachers some concern, because the following year they sent me to the Collège des Jeunes Filles, a private school for girls.

My parents had my best interest at heart when they put me in that school and never knew how I hated it. Only the daughters of Epinal's so-called elite attended the Collège des Jeunes Filles. Being the only Jewish girl in my class was bad enough, as far as they were concerned, but having Polish parents who were also merchants was unforgivable. The students' parents must have been scandalized, for they never allowed my school friends to come to my home or to invite me to theirs. The teachers were not exactly fond of me, for the same reasons, and were at times quite unfair. I couldn't explain this to my parents, of course, because at the time I did not recognize the reason for this behavior. Why did they call me a dirty Polack? I was born in France; I thought of myself as a French child. The school's principal, however, took a particular and friendly interest in me. She suggested to Papa that I should join the Girl Scouts. Maman was against it, but join I did. I loved scouting and excelled in everything related to it. I made good friends among the other scouts, who were not like the snobs I met at school.

I was an only child for a long time, a condition that I resented. Ida had a little sister, Jeannine, three years her junior, and Tante Cecile was ready to give birth to her own Jeannine. (In my family several girls were called either Jeannine or Ida after my maternal grandmother or the deceased Baron sister.) It is possible that Maman, because she had had such a hard time giving birth to me, feared having another baby. Whatever her reasons were, no one discussed them with me or in front of me. (The subject of a second baby may have been the cause of the only fight I remember my parents having. Maman was shocked when I took Papa's part in the argument without even knowing precisely what that argument was about. Whatever it was, perhaps Papa was in the right; even our housekeeper was on Papa's side.)

All I knew was that I wanted a baby in our house. On July 5, 1938, three months after my tenth birthday, my sister was born. Papa took me for a ride in the car to announce the happy event. (As far as my parents were concerned, I wasn't supposed to have suspected anything; children in Epinal were routinely told that babies were bought at Magasin Réunis, a department store. In fact, I *did* know; a school friend had informed me.) Papa told me that he and Maman had decided to have a baby just for me because I always complained of being an only child. When I asked what they would name the baby, Papa said, "Josephine Evelyn, after my father, Joseph, and my mother." He explained to me the Jewish tradition of naming children after a deceased loved one. Josephine—the name just did not ring right. Such a long, imposing name for such a little one! I remember saying, *"Oh! Papa, pas Josephine. Je préfére Josette."* And Josette she became. I was the happiest child in town that afternoon.

I was allowed to visit Maman, who was in a posh private hospital in a doctor's town house. I was so impressed: Maman looked like a queen in that big, beautiful bed. The room was furnished in French provincial antiques, and the bassinet was pink, as were Josette's sheet, clothes, and cheeks. She was a perfect child, my blonde, blue-eyed doll. Maman said, "This is my present to you. You always wanted a sister; this way you will never be alone."

After she recuperated, Maman went back to work, so I spent most of my time at home with our housekeeper and Tante Regine. Josette was always wheeled in her portable crib to my side—while I did my homework, while I read, while I ate. I was with her more than anyone else was. It seemed only natural that the first word she spoke was my name.

My mother had a flair that the French call *un cachet* (a style). The decor of our home reflected this. One friend

[12]

of the family, a furniture store owner, used to say each time he visited our home, "Your house, madame, is a castle." Maman adored fine china and prized her collection of Baccarat and Lalique crystal and her antiques, which included many jewelry and candy boxes.

Maman's superb cooking was limited to holidays, when we always had a houseful of relatives and other guests. As for sewing, Maman occasionally designed a dress for me, but time to execute her design was limited. The family business always came first.

My studies didn't seem to concern Maman, but the concern she lacked in that area she more than made up for in others. Although we had a housekeeper, I had to learn at an early age to make my bed and to perform many household duties. A seamstress came weekly to take care of our wardrobes and to teach me to make hems and to embroider. In those days, children were not allowed to be idle. We didn't have television, of course, and we were taught to spend our free time in a constructive manner. Sometimes Maman realized that perhaps she was too demanding, and she would say kindly, "Someday, *ma chérie,* I will no longer be with you. I want to be certain that you will conduct yourself in a proper and gracious manner so that you'll be liked and respected by the people you meet. Only then will you remember and understand what I'm trying to teach you now."

Maman spoke to me so often about my life without her that I almost believe she had a premonition of things to come. Sometimes it was difficult to live up to her expectations—as difficult as it was to live up to those of my father. Maman often seemed reserved, even standoffish with Josette and me. She was, in fact, quite awkward with Josette.

Maman was poised and sure of herself with her business associates and customers, but her self-confidence was accompanied by a pronounced stubborn streak. Once she had made up her mind, that was that. One day at school I fell while ice skating during the noon recess. My nose hit the ice with a decided crack, and my head began to ache immediately. The director of the school tended to me and then sent me home with the janitor. Because Maman was at the store, the janitor told Germaine what had happened. Maman believed neither me nor Germaine. According to Maman, I had made up the story to get attention. The next morning my nose was bruised and grossly swollen. "Oh look, Germaine," she said, "her nose is different!"

Papa was more French than the French. His adopted country had everything he enjoyed: art, music, and a breathtakingly beautiful, diversified countryside. Most important of all, France had Paris. Papa would talk to me at great length about his love for *la cité des lumières*. He promised that he would take me there as soon as I was old enough to appreciate it.

Most retail business people who lived and worked *en province* (outside the capital) would travel each season to Paris to buy new merchandise. This was the one part of the business for which Papa had sole responsibility. Maman always stayed behind to mind the store. Papa was more an intellectual than a businessman. He took care of the buying and the bookkeeping, but he rarely did any actual selling. When Papa finally decided to take me on one of his buying trips, I thought I was going to heaven—and in a way I was. Maman packed a suitcase with my Sunday best and bombarded me with exhortations on how to behave. The big day finally arrived. We were to travel in style, for by then Papa owned a Citroën Traction Avant, which was considered *the* car to drive.

When we reached the outskirts of Paris, Papa told me to close my eyes. He wanted my first impression of the city to be memorable. It seemed an eternity until he told me to open my eyes. Papa had stopped the car on a hill right above the Champs de Mars, by the Trocadero, now replaced by the Museum of Modern Art. There was the Eiffel Tower in full view, and in all its glory. I was really in Paris! It was not a dream. On this trip, and on several that followed, Papa took me to all the places he had mentioned to me so frequently: Versailles, the Louvre, the theaters, the Place de la Concorde. The *pièce de résistance*, however, was the opera. Just to view the building was an experience in itself. I felt like a princess at a ball when I floated up that majestic stairway to attend a production of *La Bohème*.

I think Papa had as much fun as I had on those trips. It was indeed a privilege to have him for even such a short time. He taught me to appreciate so many things.

Around the mid-thirties, when it became apparent that Hitler was not going to go away and that Jews were no longer welcome in Germany, many German-Jewish refugees came to Epinal, among other cities in our region and elsewhere in France.

Epinal is in eastern France, only a short distance from Germany. The arrival of the refugees in our town made a marked impression on me. My parents were visibly concerned, and the situation was a major topic of conversation in our household. Some refugees arrived with the clothes on their backs; others were able to bring their small, portable valuables. Nevertheless, all had to leave everything they had worked for in Germany: their homes, their work, and their way of life.

Foreigners in France were required to apply for working papers before they sought employment. These papers were not easily obtained, especially with the influx of refugees. Together with Epinal's other Jewish leaders Papa formed a committee to assist the refugees as they arrived. After that, we always had at least one refugee at our dinner table. One, a tall, lean man named Hans, stayed with us until he was able to emigrate to the United States. He took quite an interest in me. I taught him some French; in return he taught me some German. He also helped my parents with their business.

Papa had given up on organized religion, mostly because he thought it created division and bigotry among people. No one was prouder to be Jewish than Papa, but he chose his friends from all walks of life; their religion had no bearing on his feelings for them. Papa's best friend, Jean Aubert, wanted Papa and Maman to be his daughter's godparents, and both men were thoroughly mystified when Jean Aubert's church objected. When someone who happened to be Jewish made the headlines, Papa, bursting with pride, made a point of mentioning it to me. He told me to be proud of my heritage, that the only way to fight discrimination was to asssimilate oneself into the country in which one lived, to be tolerant of others in order to be tolerated. As Hitler grew more powerful, Papa warned me, "If someone questions you about your religion, just answer, 'I am a human being.' " He knew then, I suppose, that at some time in the near future I might have to lie about my religion in order to save my life. Many times, and for many years afterward, I quoted him when I was asked what my religious preference was. It was, to say the least, disturbing for a young child to think that a person could be hated and abused because of religion, especially when it was a religion that person did not practice. I started to wonder if perhaps there was something wrong with us that we were hated by so many people.

I don't know if Maman, who was raised in a relatively religious home (but a much less orthodox one than Papa's), decided to stop attending religious services because of Papa's influence. She was a strong-willed woman, so I assume that she made her own choice. As I recall, none of my aunts or their families ever attended services. I never attended services in a synagogue until I came to America; yet I believe I was raised by the most religious, kind, and tolerant of parents. Papa told me time and again, "If you have but two francs and someone comes your way who has nothing, give him one franc. Never turn your back on someone you can help."

It might seem that I am painting a picture of two saintly people. My parents were human, and I am certain they had their shortcomings. But there are so many good things to say about my parents: I owe everything that is good in me to them.

Tante Regine, who supervised our household, was as important a part of my childhood as my parents were. Tantes Cecile and Brigitte figured prominently, too, but Tante Regine was my idol. I was secure in her love for me, and I returned that love unreservedly. We enjoyed an unusually close rapport. She never had to scold me, because I never gave her reason to. Tante Regine left us only when she took vacations with friends.

We spent our own vacations away from Epinal. I recall the summer my parents rented a house in a small village well known for its cheese—Le Tholly—located between Epinal and Gérardmer high in the Vosges mountains. We had spent summers there before, but this time we rented a house on a hill overlooking the village. From there we could see the cheese factory and, beyond, a great cascade—no Niagara Falls, but a tourist attraction just the same.

My parents did not come to the house every day, as I recall, but probably one evening during the week and on weekends, when many friends also came to visit. I spent most of my time with Tante Regine. She took me for long walks in the forest every day. Like Papa, she used to chat with me about everything under the sun, and I always felt comfortable with her.

Tante Regine once became very ill and had to go to a sanatorium somewhere in the Pyrenees. She was away for what seemed like forever. During her absence I became ill myself and had to be hospitalized in the Clinique du Docteur Hainault, a private hospital located in the doctor's house. The patients' rooms bore not even a remote resemblance to the usual hospital room. I stayed there so long that I still can describe my room in detail. Because I was so ill, Papa, Maman, and Germaine took turns sitting by my bedside. It was then that Papa sketched the portrait of me that later hung in our house.

I guess Tante Regine was informed of the gravity of my illness; when she learned that a specialist from Paris had been summoned to assist my own doctor, she came home. Papa picked her up at the station, and she insisted on visiting me first. The sight of her made me feel warm all over, especially when she murmured through her tears, "Itichy, Itichy" (a term of endearment used by the family). She had brought me a present, my first phonograph. Like most European children in those days, we had few toys, and so this gift had a great impact on me. In the days that followed and until I was ready to return home, Tante Regine spent most of her time at my bedside.

[18]

The brother of my maternal grandfather emigrated to the United States and lived with his family in Detroit. When I was fully recovered, Tante Regine decided to visit them and take in the 1938 New York World's Fair. I was very upset when we said our good-byes. I can still hear her: "I am only going on vacation, my dear; I will be back soon. Don't cry." The war broke out in Europe shortly thereafter, and Tante Regine was unable to return to France, a turn of events that probably saved her life.

In 1938, the year Josette was born, Hitler's army attacked Czechoslovakia and then Danzig in Poland. As the talk of impending war buzzed louder and louder in Epinal, the French began to take precautionary measures. Papa began to tell us about some of his experiences during World War I, when he was a young boy. I was fascinated by his stories. I was barely ten, and in my child's mind I hoped we would have a war; war seemed so exciting, so full of adventure. Unfortunately, my childish hopes became reality: in 1939 France and Germany declared war. Papa, for many years a naturalized French citizen, was mobilized, and Maman stayed with us and tended the business.

Maman was concerned about our welfare. In fact, she was so worried that she placed Josette in a "nana's" home on the outskirts of Epinal, only a few kilometers away, where she would be safe if the town were bombed. But I had to attend school, so I remained at home with Maman.

We were given gas masks, which we wore during air-raid practice. They smelled almost as bad as the gas they were to protect us from. Public bomb shelters, in cellars, were designated in each neighborhood. The war escalated so quickly that there was little time for adequate preparations. All windowpanes were painted dark blue, and the streetlights were never lighted. These measures were taken so that at night the German planes could not detect our towns from the air. They managed very well, however, in spite of our blackout measures. Policemen carried flashlights at night, and after sundown Epinal appeared lonely indeed.

We went out only when it was absolutely necessary. I believe there was a curfew, and the streets were patrolled not only by policemen but also by volunteer civilians who checked every home for light leakage and assisted the townspeople into the shelters during raids. Many things were requisitioned by defense forces: trucks, some cars, even horses, and all items that would be useful to the army. At that time no one doubted that, with everyone's cooperation, we would beat the "Boches" and win the war.

I missed Papa. Without him, the atmosphere at home had changed completely. Josette was at the home of "Maman" Marie Collins. Maman and my aunts seemed always to wear preoccupied looks. Uncle Albert went to war shortly after Papa. So far, war was not quite so exciting as I had anticipated.

When Maman Marie came to our home to be interviewed for her position as nana, or nanny, to Josette, she claims she fell in love with her charge at first sight. Josette was a beautiful and most endearing baby. Maman Marie was in her late thirties at that time and had already raised many children for other people. (I believe she raised some thirty in her lifetime.) She loved them all, but she always said that she never loved any quite as much as she loved Josette. Her entire family—La Mémé, her mother; Papa Auguste; and her only child, Guiguite (short for Marguerite), who was about seventeen at that time—shared that sentiment. I fell in love with each and every one of the Collinses and often stayed at their home on school holidays to be closer to Josette, whom I missed terribly.

Maman Marie was as good as she was hardworking. Her wholesome face, with apple cheeks and sparkling eyes, was typically French. Her reddened hands were the badge of a working-class French housewife. Papa Auguste, a big, strong man, was the quiet type, but when he spoke, everyone listened. Guiguite was the older sister I never had, and I was the younger sister she had always wanted. I must admit I resented Maman Marie's preference for Josette, but I loved being around her, in any case. She was so jovial and full of funny family anecdotes. She rarely left her house and gardens unless it was absolutely necessary, and she always seemed happy doing whatever she was doing. She was loved by everyone who knew her.

Papa came home for a short furlough from nearby Alsace where he was stationed. My elegant father wore a mismatched government-issued uniform: unhemmed blue slacks, a khaki coat two sizes too large, and shoes that didn't match. He made quite an issue of his "ensemble" and intended to have a uniform made to order as soon as possible. Papa, who was assigned to an antiaircraft division, complained that the ammunition did not fit the machine guns; that, he feared, spelled disaster. His concern seemed to me obsessive: all he talked of was the unpreparedness of his division. Only now can I fully appreciate his worry.

Tante Brigitte and her family decided to move to southern France. As far as they were concerned, Germany was too close to Epinal for comfort in the event of an invasion. Several other Jewish families followed in their footsteps; to Papa and Maman, however, a move was unthinkable. It was tantamount to admitting that France could possibly be invaded.

The French had hated the Germans for centuries; as children in school we were taught to hate them.

But the Jews in France were scared. They had heard rumors of the atrocities committed in Germany against Jews who had not fled. Tante Brigitte begged Maman and Tante Cecile to leave Epinal. But both Papa and Uncle Albert were in the army, stationed nearby, and Maman and my aunt did not want to be far away from them. So, we remained in Epinal. We were constantly on the alert, running to bomb shelters during day and night raids. Epinal, which had many army posts and an airport, was bombed—though not too severely—several times. We were alerted so many times during the day that it seemed as if we spent more time in the shelter than in the classroom. We eventually became accustomed to daytime raids, but we never got used to being shocked into wakefulness at night by the terrifying scream of the siren, and we never accepted having to run in the darkness to the bomb shelter. Sometimes we were alerted twice during the same night. We were fortunate to have a shelter just across the street. Everyone huddled there in an orderly manner. All in all, our shelter had a friendly atmosphere. People who ordinarily would have no reason to speak were cordial and kind to one another. For once in our lives we had a common denominator: fear.

News of the war was grim. In the late spring of 1940 the French and English armies began to retreat. The main arteries out of Epinal, going west and south, were chock-a-block with retreating soldiers. To whom, to what were they retreating? Their regiments had all dispersed. Some soldiers were wounded, some rode in trucks, most were on foot, but all were weary and, unbeknown to them, were soon to be taken prisoners of war.

Tante Cecile had started to take driving lessons but had not yet obtained her license. At the news of the invasion, with the German army practically at our door, she and Maman decided it was time for us to leave. Tante Cecile asked Maman to take cousin Jeannine in our car—Maman was an expert driver—and said she would follow us. I assume they needed both cars for our belongings.

When we reached the main road, we stopped, stunned. Everyone was running away! Some were in cars, others in trucks. Even horse-drawn carriages were in evidence. Many traveled on foot and carried their most valuable possessions. There were no express highways in France at the time. The most heavily traveled roads were called *routes nationales* and were the equivalent of the large two-lane roads in the United States. Certainly the French roads were inadequate for this exodus.

I sat in the back seat and looked out the window in amazed silence. In addition to the civilians on foot and in trucks, there were many soldiers. We had to leave our car from time to time to huddle in roadside ditches, where we were somewhat sheltered from the German planes overhead. Many people were wounded; some died. At one point we lost sight of Tante Cecile, who fortunately had taken a friend and her friend's daughter along. Maman was worried, but there was no way we could stop and wait for Cecile; we had to roll along steadily to avoid holding up the incredible number of vehicles following us. At times we were all but standing still in huge traffic jams. Many people abandoned malfunctioning cars and continued on foot. Fortunately, Maman had had the good sense to fill the tank and bring along some cans filled with gas. The fields on either side of us were dotted with vehicles that could not find space on the road itself.

I don't recall any hysteria, even when the planes whined insistently overhead. It is generally thought that tragedy has a way of bringing out the best in most people. I know this to be true. There was a heavy weight of sadness present, a cloud of gloom, a gnawing fear that the world as we knew it was coming to an end. The early summer weather and the hot, bright sun did nothing to dispel the darkness within us. But with this fear came courage and a sense of fellowship.

At one point Maman assisted a young woman in labor on the side of the road. Maman certainly seemed competent. At least the young mother-to-be thought so. Maman's two difficult labors had taught her patience with and compassion for the laboring mother. When the baby emerged, healthy and hearty, Maman looked as pleased as if she had just given birth herself. Along the way, Maman stopped to help many wounded people and give rides to several faltering older people.

I don't remember how many days it took us, but we finally reached a small village near Vichy in the Puy-de-Dôme region in central France where Maman thought we would be safe. Tante Cecile had not caught up with us, and we had no idea where she was. This was, of course, an added concern for Maman.

In the main plaza of the village stood a church and a school, both of which the villagers had turned into shelters to house the refugees. It was exceedingly crowded, so Maman went from house to house in the village until she persuaded a kind woman, the owner of a dry goods store, to rent us two rooms. Maman slept in one room with Josette, then two years old; Jeannine, who was three, and I shared the other. We were allowed to use the main

[24]

kitchen. Because she shared my room, Jeannine was my responsibility. She had grown dependent on me since she had been separated from her mother. All of a sudden, at the age of twelve I was expected to act grown up. Maman told me that she depended on me to help her with the children. She spoke to me as if I were her equal; we were like two adult women taking care of their toddlers. Each day I walked to nearby farms for milk and provisions. It was a sad time in history for France, but among much of its population there developed a solidarity that lasted until the war was over.

The refugees gathered at the school every day to listen to the radio for news. We had no idea of Papa's or Tante Cecile's whereabouts, but we prayed that they were alive and safe.

Finally, we heard that France had surrendered to the German Reich. Our English allies, those who had not been captured as POWs, had retreated to Great Britain. There in that school, we experienced anguished feelings of helplessness, feelings that we shared with every citizen in France. We stayed in the village for another week, and then Maman decided to return to Epinal, where she assumed Papa and Tante Cecile would look for us. Maman was worried about what she would find upon returning home, and she expressed her fears to me as if I were an adult. I didn't know it then, but I was well on my way to becoming a woman.

Driving north, we saw some of the occupation forces. The sight of my first German was very frightening, but Maman was even more fearful. She paled visibly when she saw the soldier, but her determination to go home to find her husband and sister was stronger than her fear.

We finally drove up our street, relieved to see that our house was still standing, though it had been damaged by explosives when the retreating French soldiers blew up nearby bridges to slow down the German army. When we got out of the car, one of our neighbors ran out to tell us that our apartment was occupied by some Alsatian refugees. Our lodgers had made themselves quite at home, even going so far as to wear some of my parents' clothing. They did not apologize, and they made no effort to leave. Maman explained to me that it was best not to make a fuss. She was obviously afraid of the Germans and didn't want to attract any attention to herself. But I remember that she cried during the night. When our uninvited guests left two weeks later to return to their homes, many of our belongings disappeared, and the house was a shambles. The day after we returned to Epinal, Maman took Josette and Jeannine to Maman Marie (on whose care of Josette she had grown to rely), who told us that Papa had come there looking for us on the very evening we left. Maman Marie and Papa Auguste had pleaded with him to stay at their home, but Papa said he had to rejoin his regiment. The children remained at Maman Marie's, and Maman and I went home to resume some semblance of living.

Epinal was near many army posts, and Maman was told that the posts housed prisoners of war who were being kept there until they could be shipped to Germany. There were so many of them, French and English, that the Germans had to build camps in Germany to house them. Maman and I went to inquire at each *caserne* (army post), hoping that perhaps Papa was there.

Papa's name was not on the list of POWs, but Maman noticed the name of a friend, Mr. Aspis. The prisoners were allowed visitors once a day, so we asked to see him. He was glad to see two familiar faces. He didn't know where his wife and children were, but I think the sight of us buoyed his hopes for their safety. Maman hoped that he had seen Papa at one time or another, but he hadn't.

Mr. Aspis's main complaint was that the prisoners were starving. So, every day thereafter I took him food that Maman prepared. It was a long walk from our home to the camp, but I didn't mind, as I could see that my visit was the high point of Mr. Aspis's day. His usually somber expression brightened when he spotted me among the crowds of visitors. Maman often said that she hoped someone would return the kindness to Papa wherever he was. Then she would sit wordlessly for a while, tears filling her eyes, and I knew that she wondered, as I did many times, if he was still alive.

I continued to take food daily to Mr. Aspis for at least a month. He swore that he would never forget Maman and me for as long as he lived. Maman never returned to the post after her first visit; it was too painful for her. We still had no news from Papa, and Maman was growing increasingly worried. One day I went to the camp as usual, but our friend was not in the visitors' room. Maman thought perhaps he was sick, so she asked me to return the next day, and the next, but I did not see him again. We found out later that Mr. Aspis had escaped with several other prisoners.

One day Maman met a dear old friend whose husband had been killed in the war. They decided to go into business together. The Nazis had given all Jewish stores to French Gentiles, who managed the stores for a modest salary and turned over their profits to the Germans. The Jews had no control over their own stores: they weren't even allowed inside. Obviously, Maman and her friend could not have their own store. Instead, they drove to factories in the surrounding areas, and occasionally to Paris, to buy merchandise that they would then resell to retail stores and merchants. Maman had made many connections during her days as a *marchand forain* with Papa, so the business eventually did extremely well.

Maman was more beautiful than ever, but her expression was always sad. Life at home had changed completely: my aunts and cousins weren't there now, and Papa's absence left an emptiness that was hard to accept. Maman had her work, and I was often left alone. I returned to school, but I was unhappy because of the fearful atmosphere at home and in the whole city. I missed Papa and wondered if I would ever see him again.

My frequent visits to Maman Marie's, where the household remained cheerful, boosted my flagging spirits. When Maman had to travel, I would stay at the Collinses overnight, and I often wished I didn't have to go home. Josette and Jeannine were always so happy to see me, and Guiguite and I had fun together. The Collinses lived in Chantraine, a residential area where one rarely saw a German soldier. The Nazis imposed certain rules and regulations on the population, but, by and large, French citizens were left pretty much alone at that time, and some of the French started to relax. Many began to voice the opinion that the Germans weren't as bad as the French had anticipated. But it was only the calm before the storm.

Food was rationed by then, and I often stood on line for our meager allotment. We were given food coupons, which quickly became popular black-market items. With enough money one did not go hungry, but the majority of French citizens did feel the pinch. Clothing, too, was rationed, and everyone began to look shabby. The stores often ran out of food, and if I didn't get in line early in the morning I didn't always get our ration for the day. There were no supermarkets at the time, so I had to shop in specialty stores. Lines were everywhere; they became a way of life. Checking food rumors was a popular pastime. Because butter was a thing of the past, at the news that a certain butcher was going to receive a shipment of beef suet, people would stand in line from as early as five in the morning in the hope of getting some. Wine was rationed, but since Maman didn't drink we were able to get our shoes resoled by giving our wine ration coupons to a shoemaker in exchange for his services. Eventually, however, leather became completely unobtainable, and we had to wear shoes with wooden soles.

After the German invasion, France was divided into two zones—occupied and nonoccupied (*la France libre*), the latter run by the Vichy government under Marshal Pétain. In order to go from one zone to another, one had to get a permit from the German *Kommandantur*. Jews, of course, dared not apply unless they had false papers; illegal trading of papers became a big but dangerous business. Every citizen had to register with the *Kommandantur* in his or her town. Therefore, if someone was stopped at the border with false papers, one phone call to the *Kommandantur* could bear out German suspicions, and the French citizen would be arrested and eventually deported to Germany. Consequently the French started to cross the border illegally. Permits were given only in case of emergency, so many crossed the border without them.

I do not recall how or just when we heard that Tante Cecile had settled in a town called Orange. But she soon returned to Epinal to get Jeannine, and she too had to cross the border illegally.

Several days after Tante Cecile had lost us on the road, she met a family from Epinal who knew us. They told her that they had seen our car explode and that we were all dead. Our car—a black Citroën—looked like many others. Apparently, these people had seen us on the road and later mistook a blown-up Citroën for ours. Eventually, Tante Cecile ran into someone who had just been discharged from a military hospital in Marseilles. He told Tante Cecile that Uncle Albert was still a patient there. He was suffering from shell-shock and had temporarily lost his ability to speak.

Tante Cecile begged Maman to come and stay with them in the nonoccupied zone. But since Maman was sure that Papa would look for us in Epinal, she declined, and Tante Cecile returned to Orange with Jeannine. Uncle Albert had three brothers in New York who sent them papers that would enable them to emigrate to the States.

The United States had not officially declared war on Germany, but they were our allies; hence all direct communication between the States and Germany had been stopped. And because France was now occupied by the Germans, there was no direct transportation between France and America. Tante Cecile and Uncle Albert had to go to Casablanca to book passage on a ship bound for the United States. Few ships were available, and it was one year before they were able to sail.

Finally, Maman learned that a camp for prisoners of war was located near Strasbourg, in Alsace, close to the German border. Epinal was about a ninety-minute drive from the border, so we left early the next day and prayed that Papa would be there. Josette, too young to understand, was the only cheerful passenger. Along with us rode another woman whose husband was missing. Maman drove silently, and, as we came closer to the border, the German patrols stopped us many times. Maman maintained her composure and explained why she was driving toward the border. Fortunately, they never asked to see her papers, and because she was a beautiful woman they were even rather nice to her. I can only imagine how afraid she must have been that they would know she was Jewish; our family name could not be mistaken for anything else. Maman thought it was a good omen and that we would find Papa at the camp. When we arrived I stayed with Josette while Maman and our passenger went to inquire. It was a typical camp, with wooden barracks surrounded by barbed wire, a guard tower, and armed soldiers everywhere. I could see the prisoners inside, and I kept looking through the car window, hoping to see Papa. I promised God that I would never be bad again if he would only let my Papa be there. The longer it took for Maman to return, the more optimistic I became and the more impatient with Josette, who was, after all, still a baby and getting cranky. I did not have to ask questions when they finally returned; their faces betrayed their unhappiness. Papa had been in the camp but had been shipped to Germany the week before. We considered ourselves lucky just to know that Papa was alive, however; our passenger was not as fortunate. Her husband's name was not even on the list, and she cried inconsolably all the way home.

Some time later we received a letter from Papa addressed to us in care of Maman Marie. He wasn't sure of our whereabouts and figured that Maman Marie would know and would forward his letter to us. He was in a camp somewhere in Germany. (That is all any prisoner was ever allowed to say.) He had been wounded and was not permitted to write sooner, but he was now able to correspond once a month and was allowed to receive one package from home each month. We could tell from his letter that Papa was hungry.

This was the first happy day for Maman and me since

that day in July when we had fled to the south of France. We wrote Papa and sent a package to him immediately. We had to wait impatiently for the answer, which came a month later. Papa was happy to hear that we were all well and that life went on. Maman, like many other wives and mothers, had to make the best of a bad situation. But after worrying for so long and wondering whether Papa was alive, we had a lot to be grateful for. God had answered our prayers; it took him awhile, but he had so many to answer in those days.

I don't think I learned much in school that year. Maman was more lenient than Papa in that department, although she did hire a tutor to help me.

Maman was insistent about my coming straight home from school. She worried when I was away unless she knew where I was. I usually walked home with a schoolmate who lived nearby. One day as we passed a German-occupied office building, two French prisoners who were sweeping the stoop waved to us. One asked us to get him some aspirin, and the other asked us to mail a letter. We were delighted; we felt like heroic spies, risking our lives to help French prisoners. Our delight was short-lived, however. We knew that civilians were forbidden to speak to prisoners under any circumstances, and so we were not exactly surprised to find ourselves being escorted at gunpoint by two S.S. up a steep stairway to the second floor of the building. My friend became hysterical. Strangely enough, I was not afraid, even though this was my first face-to-face encounter with a German. We were told to sit down and wait. Soon a German officer came in, and a guard took my friend to another room. The officer questioned me about what had happened between us and the prisoners, and accused me of lying, apparently convinced that I was trying to help the prisoners escape. He became quite angry when I gave the same truthful answers over and over. I remained calm, which seemed to infuriate him all the more. He insisted that I had committed a felony, that civilians were not allowed to speak to prisoners. I wondered what would happen to the prisoners. Finally, my friend, still crying, reentered the room, followed by the officer who had been questioning her. The officers spoke briefly in German and apparently came to the conclusion that we were telling the truth, as our stories jibed.

Nevertheless, my interrogator told us to remain seated in the room until he decided what punishment we deserved. It occurred to me just then that Maman would be worried. I was more angry than scared, but most of all I felt an urgent need to go to the bathroom; that kept me from worrying too much about anything else. After what seemed an eternity we were told we could go home, but we were warned that things would not go so easily if we were caught again.

They must have kept us for at least three hours. In her eagerness to get out of the building and home, my girl friend fell and rolled all the way down the steep stairway. But her bruises did not stop us from running all the way home. Maman was frantic; she screamed at me before I could explain what had happened. When she calmed down and heard my story all she could say was, "Oh, mon Dieu, mon Dieu! They could have killed you! Thank God they didn't know you were Jewish."

I never walked in front of that building again, but I would know exactly where to find it today, although I left Epinal thirty-five years ago.

That summer of 1941 marked one year that the Germans had occupied France. We exchanged letters with Papa as often as we were allowed; his letters and our visits to

Maman Marie were our emotional salvation. Josette was articulate for a child of three, so when we took her home for an occasional weekend, the house seemed more cheerful with her carefree chatter.

At the advice of my dear teacher, Miss Colin, Maman enrolled me in a private boarding school, the collège des jeunes filles (girls' high school) in Dôle (Jura), some distance from Epinal, near the Swiss border. I would be able to come home only for Christmas, Easter, and the summer holidays. That prospect did not please me, but Maman explained that it would be best for me. I would be enrolled as Jacqueline Glicen, so no one there would know I was Jewish. I would be safer, and perhaps my schoolwork would improve in a private school.

Maman and I took a train to Dôle. I was unhappy, and I wished I could order Maman to turn around and take the next train home. But I was not a child who questioned my parents' motives, at least not aloud, so I never told Maman how I hated the prospect of a separation.

The first sight of the school alarmed me. What looked like a prison to me was really an old castle, complete with moat and drawbridge. When we reached that massive door, even Maman fidgeted apprehensively, but of course she did not say a word. Maman and I met the principal, an enormous woman with haughty good looks. She asked me to wait outside her office while she spoke to Maman, and then the two of us were shown to the dormitory where I was assigned a bed and a locker. Maman helped me unpack; as we put folded clothes away she told me to be good, to remember my parents, and to write every week. Before she left, she took me in her arms and warned me to tell no one that I was Jewish. What I felt when she walked away was more than the pain any child feels when facing separation from a beloved parent. I was

[34]

angry. I hurt in my soul. I hated being Jewish. I believed I hated Maman, and, to be truthful, I *did* hate her at that moment. I hated Germans most of all, and I cried for Papa. If he had not been a prisoner of war, I wouldn't be left there; *he* wouldn't have left me there.

My stay at the school was not happy, and I have no fond memories of the place, although I do have good memories of some of the students I became friends with there. I had to have tutors in several subjects; therefore, my study hours were interminable. Weekends were lonely because most of the students lived nearby and could go home. I was the youngest of the group that remained at the school, and most of the older girls ignored me. The food was, at best, bland and, at worst, unpalatable. Mail from home made my day. Occasionally, a schoolmate would invite me to her home for the weekend for a change of scene. I returned home for Christmas and spent a happy ten days with Maman, Josette, and the Collinses. Maman told me that in his letters Papa expressed concern about my studies. I vowed to try harder when I returned to school to please him.

On the trip between home and school I had to change trains in Belfort, with a layover of two and a half hours. I spent the time visiting with dear friends of my parents who lived in town. I always enjoyed spending these few hours with them.

When I went home for the Easter holiday I looked forward to seeing them again, but they were not as cheerful as usual when they greeted me. I noticed a badge sewn on their clothing: a yellow and black Star of David with the word *Juif* written within the star. I was flabbergasted; I had no idea Jews had to wear a star. Maman had not mentioned it in her letters, and no one wore them in Dôle. At any rate, I had never seen anyone wearing one while on my weekly walk with the school group. The realization hit me—like a punch in the stomach—that things could only grow worse. But would they ever be better?

On the train from Belfort to Epinal, Jewish stars danced in my mind's eye, and I wondered if Maman was wearing one. When I arrived in Epinal Germaine, our housekeeper, met me at the station. She handed me a coat and told me to wear it instead of the one I had on. When I questioned her, she replied with some embarrassment in her voice that those were Maman's orders. Then I saw the black Star of David on a gold cloth with the black-lettered *Juif* in the middle.

Maman was not at the station to meet me, because Jews had to observe a curfew. I was to keep my train stub handy to prove why I was out so late in case we were stopped by the gestapo. I felt as if suddenly I had become a leper. I resented Germaine who, because she was a Gentile, was all of a sudden—at least in the minds of many thousands of Germans—my moral, intellectual, and racial superior. I felt branded for all the world to see, for all the world to say, "Look at her, she belongs with the scum of the earth. She is a Jew."

Fortunately, few people were walking in the streets that evening. Nevertheless, those I did come across stared, probably because I was out late in the evening after curfew. Of course I thought that they were looking down at me and thinking, "Oh, a Jew." The walk from the station to our house usually took no more than ten or fifteen minutes, but, although we walked quite briskly, this time the walk seemed to take forever.

Maman was so bubbly when I arrived that I almost forgot the long walk home. Papa had been repatriated into nonoccupied France. He was still recovering from his wounds in a hospital in Perpignan, near the Spanish border. Tante Cecile and Uncle Albert had gone to visit him and had reported that he soon would be well, at which time he was supposed to be discharged and freed. This wonderful news gladdened me.

I believe that in the nonoccupied zone at the time one could make contact with people in the United States, perhaps through the Red Cross or through people who had contacts in Spain or Portugal. There surfaced a number of despicable people, however, who for large sums of money promised to perform miracles—anything from obtaining caviar to guiding fleeing Jews across the Pyrenees into the safety of Spain. Many were thieves who left Jews stranded in those mountains, robbed of their jewels and money. There were, of course, many, many French citizens who risked their lives to help Jews; those who made their living "helping" Jews were few in comparison.

I do not know how Papa got in touch with his family in the States, but he did, and he asked them to send him the papers necessary to get us out of France through Africa. Tante Cecile and her family were leaving shortly, and Papa was to take over their house and store in Orange. We would join him in July and live there until we could depart for the United States. It would not be easy; we would have to cross the border clandestinely, but Maman had already made connections. All this would take time. Because so many people were crossing illegally, the Germans tightened their surveillance and shot many people on sight at the border. Josette would cross with a Gentile woman who specialized in taking children into the nonoccupied zone. They would travel by train. The woman had a pass that enabled her to cross the border without being questioned. Children under five did not require papers, so Josette, who would be four in July, would pose as the woman's own child.

The Germans repatriated and discharged Papa because he had been wounded and was still recuperating. The Germans wanted only healthy people who were able to work hard. Therefore, they mobilized young Frenchmen in exchange for the injured prisoners who were of no use to the Nazis. (Actually, when Papa was in camp, the Germans did not know that he was Jewish; he had burned all his identification papers.) So, during that period, many young men fled into nonoccupied France in order to escape labor camps in Germany and with the hope of reaching Africa in order to join the Free French army.

I had not seen Papa for over two years. I was to return to school and stay until mid-July, which marked the beginning of the summer holdiays. We would leave that same week to rejoin Papa in Orange; he was not allowed to return to the occupied zone.

During the Easter holiday I spent much of my time at Maman Marie's. I was happy to see Josette, who glowed with health and happiness; she was too young to be aware of the changes in Epinal.

Jews had a curfew in the early evening and were allowed to shop only during certain hours in the daytime. Shop owners were forbidden to wait on us at any other time, although many did. One day, Maman and I entered a store ten minutes late, and the owner, who had known us for a long time, refused to wait on us. At first Maman pleaded that she needed only one item. The shopkeeper was adamant, and she actually took us by our elbows and propelled us out of the store. I was humiliated enough by having to wear the star, but this was intolerable. Maman was more furious than embarrassed. As she walked out the door she said, "The war will not last forever, madame, and someday you will regret this action."

Another Nazi rule required Jews to step off the sidewalk into the gutter to allow German soldiers to pass. Maman, a proud woman, had never complied with such a ridiculous regulation and had never been reprimanded. Maman was a strikingly elegant lady; perhaps even German Jew-haters were impressed by her lofty demeanor. One day, however, she and I passed an S.S. soldier who ordered us in French to step down; Maman simply ignored him and walked on. Furious, he shoved her to the ground. Coolly, she got up, took my hand, and started to walk again. He pushed her again, a little harder this time, and shrieked at her in German, "You are a Jewish pig." By then, a crowd had formed around us. Maman got up again with the help of a French gentleman, stepped back on the sidewalk, took my hand again, and told me to stop crying. I guess the crowd intimidated the German, who walked away, trying to appear unruffled. Maman's coat was soiled, her stockings were torn, and her knees were trickling blood. We walked home, crying silently. I resented being Jewish more than ever that day, but at the same time felt guilty about that resentment.

On April 28, I celebrated my fourteenth birthday. I thought, with hope, that the nightmare couldn't last much longer. There was so much to look forward to: a safe life in the United States, where Jews did not have to wear stars and fear for their lives; seeing Tante Regine again. During the remaining two and a half months of school the days and the weeks dragged by, but Papa's letters of encouragement calmed my impatience.

Finally, the last day of school arrived, and I stopped in Belfort as always. When I arrived at our friends' home, I noticed strange papers, emblazoned with swastikas, pasted all over the door. Although I spoke and under-stood German well, I couldn't read the printed German alphabet, but I recognized the word *Jude*. No one an-swered when I rang the bell, but eventually a neighbor came out and told me matter-of-factly, "Oh, the Jews were all picked up by the gestapo a few days ago." The Nazis had sealed our friends' apartment, and the notice on the door warned that anyone who broke the seals would be imprisoned. The seals would remain on the door until the Nazis removed the contents of our friends' home. My mind reeling, I walked back to the train sta-tion, my stomach churning. I felt the nausea that intense fear often produces. Would I find the same seals on our front door? Had they taken Maman away?

When I arrived in Epinal I was relieved to see Ger-maine, who rushed me home. The gestapo had not taken Maman away, she told me as we walked home, but Maman was in the hospital, where she was recuperating from an operation. Papa had been informed of Maman's illness and could no longer stay away. He was expected late that evening.

When he arrived, his appearance alarmed me. He was so thin; his hair was so white. I was almost surprised that he was able to hold me in his arms for so long and with all his old strength. I told him about our friends in Belfort, about my fear for our family. He told me not to worry be-cause we would be leaving in the morning. We would pick up Josette and hide for a few days on a farm until Maman was ready to leave the hospital.

Papa and I spent much of the night packing. A friend of ours, Mr. Henriot, was to come at six o'clock in the morning to drive us to Maman Marie's.

In my parents' bedroom there was a traditional French armoire with a mirrored double door. In the frenzied activity of packing, Papa somehow broke the mirror. "Bad luck!" he cried. Papa was upset and knew, perhaps, that with or without the broken mirror, we were in for some bad luck.

Early in the morning, we went to bed. A short time later I was awakened by a loud knocking on the door. I jumped out of bed to open the door, thinking it was Mr. Henriot. To my horror, it was the gestapo: two German civilians, three armed soldiers, and a Frenchman from the Police Secrete who knew my father well. They pushed me aside and began to search the house. At that moment I knew that we were going to be arrested. I ran to Papa's room where he was dressing, his face drained of color and his hands trembling so that he couldn't button his shirt. He asked me to help, and I found myself able to do what he couldn't.

Meanwhile, the Nazis were ransacking our home, looking through all our things. Everything Papa had packed the previous night they scattered around the room. They asked Papa, "Where is your wife?" Papa just shook his head, as if he couldn't hear them, or couldn't understand. The French collaborator who accompanied the gestapo recalled that Papa always wore a watch with a gold chain on his vest. He kept saying, "Paul, where is your watch? Give it to me!" I remember Papa's incredulous and saddened look at this request. (After the war I pressed charges against this man, but dropped them when the Jews who remained in Epinal begged me to, since he was still in office and they were afraid of him.)

At one point, while the Germans were busy looking around, Papa whispered to me, "No matter how many times they ask you, don't tell them that Maman is in the hospital." Later, they hustled us out the door. Papa held back, but one of the men grabbed him and yelled,

"Hurry! Get out, Jew!" Was this actually happening to us? It seemed as if an eternity had passed since Papa had come home for the first time in two and a half years, yet it was only seven hours before. When we reached the sidewalk it seemed that in spite of the early hour every neighbor had come out to say good-bye. Some women were crying, many shouted encouraging words to us, others cursed the Germans. There were two black gestapo cars waiting for us. The Germans attempted to separate me from Papa, but I held on to him so tightly that they could not pull me away. Papa said, "Leave her alone; she is only a child." (I don't want to suggest that the Germans allowed me to go with Papa because they were moved by my tears. Never! They were fanatically indoctrinated to hate Jews so much that a Jewish child was not a child but just another Jew who must be destroyed.) The reason I was able to stay with Papa was probably that the crowd was getting larger and louder, and the Germans were more interested in taking care of the business at hand than in coping with an angry mob.

Papa and I did not speak but just held on to each other until we reached the Commissariat de Police, Epinal's central police station. We entered the main room, which was filled with uniformed policemen and plainclothesmen, most of whom knew Papa. I sensed an attitude on the part of the French police, as if they felt guilty and embarrassed to be even indirectly involved in such a situation.

Papa and I were separated and taken to small offices. An officer questioned me about Maman's whereabouts, but I told them I did not know, that my parents had had a fight and that Maman had stormed out of the house. I told the same story again and again. The gestapo officer was getting angry at his French interpreter because the

Frenchman was not insistent enough with me. All I cared about was to be reunited with Papa; I was afraid they would beat him. I was finally told I could join him in the main room. Incredible as it may seem, without consulting with each other, we had both told our interrogators the same story. Papa and I spoke for some time, but all I recall is that Papa thought we would not be released. He kept saying that if he had been able to get home sooner we would not be here. "What will happen to you, *ma chérie?*" Tears spilled down his face. Papa gave me a large sum of money and told me to hide it in my clothing and not to let anyone know I had it. He kept some in his own pocket so as not to raise suspicions in the event of a body search.

Only French policemen were in the room at the time, and they hardly spoke to us. I guess they were helpless and stunned, and I think they respected our sorrow and understood our need for those few precious moments together. A car pulled up, and then we heard footsteps coming toward us. When I looked up I almost screamed, for it was Maman, flanked by two of the gestapo. This was the first time she had seen Papa in two and a half years, and she ran over to hold him close to her. The translator waved them on, into another office, and I was left by myself, hoping we would be released. I later found out that the gestapo had questioned all our neighbors and that someone had revealed Maman's whereabouts.

As soon as my parents came out of the other room, the Germans took them out of the police station but simply ignored me. I followed and ran along with my parents. They kissed me, and Papa told me to be good and never to forget them. As a German hustled them into a parked car, Maman pushed back the Nazi who was holding her arm as if to say, "You can do what you want with me, but

[43]

I am going to kiss my child whether you like it or not." I saw reflected in her black eyes the fierce love she felt for her daughters, and then she kissed me. She kissed me with more tenderness than she had ever shown me before. As she entered the car, she turned and said, "Please take care of Josette, and don't forget your parents."

Why were they leaving? Why was I left behind? As the car drove away, I kept thinking, This is a nightmare; I *am* going to wake up. I shivered in the cold summer rain and watched the car make a right turn on to the bridge and disappear.

I knew then that the horror for me had begun. I had not said a word as I stood there on the sidewalk. I felt a hand touching me, so I looked up and met the sympathetic eyes of a young man. Around him stood many of Epinal's police officers, numb with shock. You see, my parents had another distinction: they were the first two Jews in Epinal to be arrested by the Germans. Many others would soon meet the same fate.

The young man put his arm around me and led me back into the building. It was July 13, 1942. I was too stunned to be afraid. I felt more like a robot than a young girl whose world had exploded. I sat where I was told to sit, and above the murmur of soothing voices around me I kept hearing Maman's voice: "Take care of Josette . . . take care of Josette . . . take care of Josette."

PART II

The events that followed are shadows in my memory. I don't know how long the police kept me at the station, or even what they said to me, but I remember that when I questioned the detectives, they told me that my parents would be taken to a camp called Drancy, near Paris. The Germans kept adult Jews there, the policemen told me, but not children, because it was a labor camp. The Germans wanted me to stay with some hand-picked French citizens. The police officer told me that my parents would write to me as soon as they were settled. One officer apologized, saying that he and the other French policemen had no control over what the Germans had done to my family. I found out later that in Paris and its vicinity children were arrested along with their parents. Most were killed in France and never reached the concentration camps their parents were sent to. Therefore, I always considered our survival a miracle.

At one point, two women entered the station. I recognized them immediately; they lived in the building attached to ours. In fact, they had taken over Tante Cecile's apartment when she left Epinal. The older one was a short, thin woman whose front teeth were missing. She was a cleaning woman and had assisted our housekeeper on many occasions. The heavily madeup younger woman was her daughter. She was thought to be a collaborator, because she was often seen in the company of German soldiers. The translator took the two women to another room. When they returned, he told me to go home and stay with the women. They would be responsible for me, and I was to report to the German *Kommandantur* once a week. I don't remember the women's names, but I will never forget their faces. The older woman took my hand as we left the station. I don't think I said a word to anyone.

In order to reach the women's apartment, we had to pass my family's door, on which I saw the seals with the swastika and a large padlock. I knew only too well what that meant.

At the sight of the sealed door I started to cry. The old lady tried to calm me and pull me away. Her daughter seemed annoyed by the fuss I was making and was obviously not at all happy to be my guardian.

To this day, I don't know why those two women, of all people, were chosen to look after me, unless the gestapo had some personal reasons. The daughter was a known prostitute with a police record.

I was no happier to be with them than they were to have me. The two women argued a lot, but the older one told her daughter that they had to be kind to me for my Maman's sake, because Maman had always been kind to her.

The apartment, kept immaculate, had three rooms: a large kitchen, a dining-sitting room, and a bedroom for the daughter and me. The mother slept on a cot in the adjacent dining room.

The bedroom was quite cozy, in contrast to the rest of the apartment, but was garishly furnished in twentieth-century-bordello style. Everything in the bedroom was pink: the walls, the criss-cross ruffled curtains, and the bedspread. Cheap dolls covered the bed, and on the dresser were several bottles of cheap perfume. Photos and sketches of nude women were tacked to the walls.

At one point the mother said that I wasn't going to remain with them for long, only until the Germans decided what to do with me. God alone knows how abandoned I felt on hearing that news. The selection of the two women who were to look after me served to support that feeling. In a small town like Epinal, the two women were not exactly looked upon as the crème de la crème. My parents would not approve of my being there, but they weren't in a position to do anything about it.

The women said they were forced to take me, and they told me I was to behave myself and follow their instructions. I wished I could run away to Maman Marie. The older woman revealed a glimmer of kindness when she said, "The poor kid, what will happen to her and her kind parents?"

That night, sharing the daughter's bed, I was nauseated by the smell of her heavy perfume. At one point she asked me if I was asleep. How could I be? The events of the day kept unrolling in my head like a continuous film loop. I thought I was dreaming and that I was going to wake up and all would be right with my life. I worried about Josette. I started to cry and woke up the old woman, who ran into the room. Her daughter told her to go back to sleep and then, for the first time, was quite kind. She put her arms around me and told me that everything would be all right. She murmured to me for a long time until finally I fell into a fitful sleep.

The next morning when we arose, we suddenly realized I had no change of clothes. The windows of my family's apartment faced the women's windows; our apartments were separated only by the roof of the store below. Part of the roof was glass, bordered by red clay shingles. The roof sloped down to about two feet below my family's windows. As we looked out, we noticed that our dining room window was slightly ajar. As a young child I had often climbed on the roof for fun, and Maman had punished me for it several times. So, I convinced the women to let me enter my family's apartment through the window. I was not scared at all, in spite of the seals. It was my home, and I believed I had a right to go there, no matter what the Germans said. I quickly crossed the roof and climbed into our apartment window. My suitcase, which had been carefully packed, was open; my clothes were strewn all over the place. I picked them up and threw them back into the valise. Before I left I decided to look around the house for what I thought might be the last time. I noticed the broken mirror inside the armoire and remembered Papa's saying, "Bad luck." Already it was hard to believe that we had lived there for the last ten years. The women had told me not to touch anything except my clothes because they did not want the Nazis to accuse them of stealing. On my mother's dressing table I noticed Maman's gold watch. I just had to have it, perhaps because the memory of the man who had taken Papa's watch was still so fresh. No one but I would have Maman's watch! I put it in my pocket and climbed through the window. I must have stayed longer than was necessary, because the women were calling me. The younger woman came out to help me drag the suitcase up the sloping roof. We felt like thieves and kept looking around to see if anyone was watching us.

After breakfast the older woman left for work, and her daughter told me that I was to stay all afternoon on the street in front of the building, until her "visitors" had left. She, too, had to work. Many neighbors spoke to me, most of them gravely shaking their heads, telling me how sorry they were, saying that my parents were such well-respected people.

That night, I asked the old woman if I might visit Josette the following day, but she told me not to leave their sight. I was their responsibility, she said, but perhaps Sunday she would take me there. I was an obedient child, raised to respect adults, and this time was no exception. Though I toyed with the idea of running away, I quickly pushed it out of my mind.

I played ball with the children on the block and felt guilty. My parents did not allow me to play ball, because it was not ladylike.

One afternoon, several days after my parents' arrest, I was standing on the sidewalk near our building. To my surprise, I saw my beloved Papa Auguste Collins coming toward me on his bicycle. The only person I would have been happier to see was my own Papa. I almost toppled Papa Auguste off his bike in my eagerness to see him. He picked me up and, with a touch of his warm hand, calmed me, but he was so choked up that he was unable to speak for a few minutes. After a "harumph" or two, he told me to follow his instructions carefully. "I am going to ride away," he said, "and when you see me turn the corner, start walking toward our house. Don't run, just walk normally, but fast." He was so firm that I did not question him, and as he disappeared I started to walk without looking back. My heart thumped (audibly, I was sure), and when I reached the corner, Papa Auguste was waiting for me. He sat me on the bar of his bicycle and sped toward his house, which was on a steep hill in Chantraine. At the foot of the hill, Papa Auguste usually dismounted and walked his bike up. I don't know how he summoned the strength, but this time he rode up the hill, with me sitting on the bar. Papa Auguste was not that strong a man, but he rode steadfastly. When we got to the Collinses' house, the whole family ran out to greet us and hug me. Everyone was crying, including the Thiriet family from across the street. Josette was crying, too, even though she did not really understand what had happened. I could not let go of her; for the time being, she was all I had. Maman Marie said it would be safer to go indoors. She didn't want too many people to know that Josette and I were there.

The gestapo had sent a French collaborator to inquire about Maman, to see if she was hiding in the Collinses' home. They said that they had no idea where Maman was. They were afraid that the gestapo would take Josette away, but all the Germans were concerned about was Maman. The Collinses were convinced that someone had informed the Nazis that Josette was staying at their house. Otherwise, how would the gestapo have known of their connection with our family?

A week or so after Papa Auguste came for me, a letter arrived from Papa. He had persuaded or bribed a German guard to mail it. Papa was hoping that Maman Marie knew where I was. Maman was with him, and they were hungry. They had nothing but the clothes they wore when they were arrested. Most of all, they were afraid they would be sent to Germany. Some convoys of Jews and other prisoners had already left for "the fatherland."

By that time, the Nazis were arresting Jews all over occupied France, and new prisoners were being processed in Drancy daily, including many with children. Papa and Maman were in constant fear for our safety. In Paris, Jews wearing their stars were no longer safe in the streets. The gestapo would close streets by placing armed soldiers at each end, and then they would arrest all Jews found within the barricades. Arrested, too, were some who did not wear stars but appeared to the Germans to be of Jewish extraction, according to the sound of the names on their identification papers. This sort of gestapo roundup was called a "raffle."

In Papa's letter to Maman Marie, he enclosed a letter for me in case she knew where I was. In this letter, Papa told me that I was now the head of the family, that the family's safety was in my hands. He told me where much of our money and many of our valuables were hidden and with whom. Maman had sewn some of our things inside pillows and sent them to Orange, where we had planned to reside, but the bulk was in Epinal, entrusted to some Gentile friends. Most of the people named in that letter denied ever having received anything from my parents. Jews could not put money into banks. The Nazis confiscated their bank accounts. Therefore, most Jews converted their cash to diamonds, jewelry, foreign dollars, even valuable collections, such as stamps, that they would hide or, more often than not, entrust to friends. My parents were no exception. Unfortunately, what Josette and I recouped was negligible; by the time the war was over, we were virtually destitute.

In his letter, Papa told me to send them a certain num-

[51]

ber of francs in care of an address that he included. With the money I sent, they could buy their freedom, he said. He also asked me to send a package of clothing and food to the same address. Maman had hidden some clothes in Maman Marie's attic, which also housed our dining room furniture and Maman's beautiful embroidered linens. Other people had our fine china, silver, crystal, and jewelry, as well as our money. I wasn't able to reach these people during the day, for fear of being arrested. Therefore, Mr. Thiriet would take me at night, on his motorcycle, to visit the people mentioned in Papa's letter. Although most of them denied having anything belonging to my parents, I did recover some money. Maman Marie followed Papa's instructions and sent everything he had asked for, including the money.

With enough money, even Jews could find a German to help them, and a few Jews were thus able to escape from the camp at Drancy and hide until the war was over. Others, less fortunate, were arrested again and sent to concentration camps to meet their final fate.

In his letter Papa mentioned that a cousin of Maman who lived in Lille, in northern France, would help Josette and me. I wrote to this cousin, who urged us to come as soon as possible. Mr. Thiriet took us to a train depot outside Epinal, and off to Lille we went. When we arrived at the cousin's home, I rang the doorbell. No answer. My stomach heaved with anxiety. What was I to do now? Where could my cousins be? I asked the concierge, who at first denied knowing their whereabouts, but eventually weakened and took us to another apartment in the building, where the family was hiding. The father, Maman's first cousin, had been arrested in a "raffle," and his wife and two children, fearing for their lives, had left their apartment to hide in an empty one. She was not overjoyed to see Josette and me, naturally. She was distraught; the last thing she needed was two more youngsters to be concerned with. She was not unkind, nor did she ask us to leave, but I felt uneasy. Several days later, we returned to Epinal. Our cousin's wife made no effort to discourage us from leaving. In fact, she begged me to ask Maman Marie to hide her two young sons. Maman Marie did take them; a short time later their mother was arrested and, like her husband, never returned. After the war, a wonderful couple adopted the two boys.

The Collinses had a large garden. At the end, near a pine forest, was the compost pit, piled high with horse manure. In France, every farm had such a pile; in fact, one could determine by the size of the pile the amount of land that needed fertilizing; the larger the pile, the more land the farmer owned. Therefore, the compost pit was often smack in front of the farmhouse, displayed with pride for everyone to see.

Of course Papa Auguste had only a garden, not a farm, and his compost pile was appropriately modest. He dug a trench underneath it, where Josette and I could hide if need be and where the Germans would never think to look for us. He covered the trench with a board and piled manure on top of that.

The mayor of Chantraine, whose name also was Collins, lived on the Route de Bains, which happened also to be the Collinses' street. The mayor lived halfway up the steep hill, and the Collinses lived at the top. Several days after Papa Auguste built the trench, some youngsters came running to warn us that the gestapo was ransacking the mayor's home looking for Josette and me. Seeing that their last name was Collins, the gestapo mistook them for our benefactors. Josette and I hid in the trench, and Papa Auguste covered the lid with horse manure, as planned. It was the end of August and still hot and humid. Fear, as it so often does, sharpened my senses. The odor of manure was heavy and, at such close range, nauseating. Josette began to cry, and I had to cover her mouth and hold her tight to my breast to smother the noise. Oh, God, I thought, if I vomit I'll have to let go of Josette, and then she'll scream. It was so hot and I was so frightened that it was hard for me to reassure Josette. We couldn't hear anything at first, but eventually we heard footsteps in the garden and loud German voices. My heart was pounding, and I was afraid the Germans would hear Josette's cries. I begged her to be still and kept my hand on her mouth. Finally, all was quiet. I thought I heard cars leaving, but I wasn't sure. It seemed an eternity had passed when I heard footsteps coming in our direction; it was Guiguite, who whispered, "All clear." For our own safety, she told us to stay a little longer in case the Boches decided to come back. It was almost dark when we were rescued from our hiding place and hustled into the Thiriets' home across the street. If the Germans returned, they wouldn't think to look for us there.

The Collinses decided that the time had come for us to leave the area; it was no longer safe. The Thiriets had cousins who owned a farm about fifteen kilometers away. Everyone was sure we would be safe there temporarily. That night, Mr. Thiriet drove Josette and me on his motorcycle to their relatives' home. Being patriotic, the Thiriets' cousins were happy to keep us as long as necessary.

Meanwhile, Maman Marie, who rarely left her neighborhood unless it was to attend a wedding or a funeral, put on her Sunday best to seek some advice from Maman's friend, Mrs. Henriot, who volunteered to locate some of our relatives in the nonoccupied zone. I would have to sneak across the border. Josette would go with a *passeur*, someone who had legitimate papers. (As I mentioned before, children under five years did not require papers.)

Meanwhile, the whole Collins family took turns visiting us at the farm. The Thiriet family—Jacqueline, who was a dear friend to both Guiguite and me; Raymond, her brother; and of course Mr. and Mrs. Thiriet—came, too.

Mrs. Henriot located Maman's cousins, the Rosembergs, who lived with their five children on an estate they owned in Bollène, some twenty kilometers from Orange. A short time later we received a letter from Henri, the oldest son, saying that if there was no other alternative, we should by all means try to get across. They would be glad to take us in. Mrs. Henriot found someone who had connections at the border and who would help me get across. Josette would go with the *passeur*.

Shortly before my departure, Maman Marie received a letter from Papa. He was disappointed because he thought we had not followed his instructions. (Apparently his "friendly" contact had kept the money we sent as well as the letters and packages.) He wrote unkind words to me, which made me feel sad and guilty for many years. Papa repeated the same instructions, thinking that perhaps his first letter had not reached Maman Marie. (He knew Josette and I were all right and at her home, because our cousin from Lille who had been arrested had ended up in my parents' camp in Drancy, and had told them about us.) Papa practically begged for the money, so that he and Maman could buy their freedom. Maman Marie was at a loss; to send money to the same address would be a waste of time, since the person on that end was obviously a thief. Nevertheless, we decided to try

[55]

again, since we hoped (with very little faith) that perhaps the first letter and package had been lost. Maman Marie and Papa Auguste felt it was worth taking another chance just to feel that we had left no stone unturned. Papa begged the Collinses to take good care of Josette and me. They were still in Drancy and had no idea how long they would remain there. So far, Maman and Papa had remained together.

Mrs. Henriot's friend came to the farm to tell me where to go and whom to contact once I reached the border. I was glad to leave the farm. Although the Thiriets' cousins were nice and compassionate, Josette and I had to stay indoors at all times so as not to attract the attention of outsiders. I couldn't wait to be in southern France where Jews didn't have to wear stars and were still relatively free. I hated to leave Josette behind; she was to follow in two weeks with a couple who would take her as far as Limoges. Fortunately, Mr. and Mrs. Gertler, friends of my parents, lived there, and she was to be taken to their home. If I crossed the border safely I would fetch her there. The Gertlers would advise the Rosembergs of her arrival.

Mr. Thiriet came to my rescue again and drove me to Golbey, a small town near Epinal, where I boarded the train. Most trains had been requisitioned by the occupation troops, and civilians were allowed to use them only when there was room aboard. The majority of the passengers on this particular train were German soldiers, and I tried in vain to find a compartment filled with civilians. I finally settled for a seat near a Frenchman, but I was surrounded by six soldiers and was very ill at ease. I was well developed for my age, and the looks I was getting from the soldiers were not exactly brotherly, nor were the remarks that they exchanged. After two years of occupation and being forced to study German in school, I spoke and understood the language quite well. I sat in a corner and was afraid to look up. The soldiers were drinking and were becoming loud and boisterous. One, seated directly across from me, stared openly. He had piercing eyes and kept asking me questions in German. I ignored him and acted as if I did not understand. A girl of fourteen traveling by herself was bound to attract attention, and I was terrified that the gestapo would question me when they came to check our papers. The ride from Golbey to my destination seemed interminable. Every German who looked at me was a threat. I was certain they suspected that I was about to cross the border illegally, especially the soldier who kept staring at me. There was nothing soft or kind about him; his expression was suspicious. When I arrived at my stop I was quite relieved to note that he remained on the train.

When I left the station, my fears returned. I noticed that the streets were crowded with Germans. The village was at the border and was, of course, heavily guarded. My legs were cotton, my heart was a jackhammer, and I began to perspire heavily. I was sure that every soldier who looked at me was aware of my plans, the plans of a wobbly-legged, sweaty, shifty-eyed J-e-w. It was a relatively small village and everyone seemed to know everyone else. I assumed that I looked conspicuous, but my fears were magnified by my anxiety about crossing the border.

I had been given the address of a café at the corner of the main plaza. I located it easily, without having to ask anyone for directions. It was dinnertime when I entered, and the noisy café was full of civilians and soldiers having dinner or just drinking. I walked straight to the bar and asked for the man I was to contact; he owned the establishment and was also the bartender. I was so glad to meet him that, without thinking, I spilled out, perhaps in too loud a voice, my reason for being there. The poor man's face drained of color, and he hushed me. Finally, since I was insistent, he quite angrily told me he never heard of such foolishness and that I was obviously in the wrong place. He said I must stop telling nonsensical stories or I would get him into trouble. Then I realized that we were surrounded by soldiers who, fortunately, were not paying attention to us and who didn't understand French anyway. Only then did I realize my blunder.

The man's wife ushered me to a nearby table and told me to sit there for a while. She brought me some food and told me to eat slowly and act as if I had come in to have dinner. Now, the average fourteen-year-old girl did not eat in restaurants by herself—not in those days—so I was sure to attract attention. What was I to do now? The man had told me that I was mistaken, that he didn't know what I was talking about. I was a wreck. I ate my food mechanically, with my head down. I was afraid to meet anyone's eyes for fear that I would be questioned, and I was afraid to get up to go to the bathroom, even though my bowels rumbled menacingly, a situation that often occurred when I was anxious. I was in torment sitting there. I had two problems to cope with, and as the latter one became unbearable, I finally got up and ran to the bathroom. I stayed there for quite a while, afraid to return to the dining area.

I knew I was at a point of no return: I couldn't go back to Epinal, but the man here had told me I was in the wrong place. They had not chased me out, however, and that left me with some hope. Most cafés in France had but one bathroom for both men and women, and finally someone pounded on the door, forcing me to depart. Just then, a young woman signaled me to come through the back into the kitchen where the *patron* (owner) was waiting for me. He seemed angrier than before and raved on for quite some time until I was able to explain. He kept saying, "You could have had us all shot with your blabbering." He did have an excitable nature, but in those circumstances he was justified in reacting as he did. He calmed down at the insistence of his wife, who said to him, "Calm down! She is a kid." I explained through my tears what had happened to me in the last two months, since that fateful thirteenth day of July.

The café was a family business, managed by both the parents and their two daughters. I was told to stay in the kitchen until closing time when they would deal with me. Probably the only café in the relatively small village, this one, like most cafés in France, not only offered food but also served as a gathering place for the men in the town. There they passed time over drinks with their friends, so the café closed quite late.

I was so tired that evening that I fell asleep at the kitchen table. The older daughter woke me and took me upstairs. I was to share her bedroom, and there she assured me that everything would look brighter in the morning. No one had said anything about crossing the border, but I felt optimistic because they kept me overnight, so I didn't question her. Besides, after such a long and strenuous day, I was glad to go to bed and stop thinking.

The next morning, I ate breakfast with the family, and they told me they would deal with me after the lunch hour was over. If I wanted to, I could help out in the kitchen to occupy myself. Everyone was so friendly, especially the young girl whose room I had shared. She was about nineteen. The time flew by; it was a busy kitchen. I had not noticed the night before that the grandparents did the cooking; the parents and the two daughters served the customers in the main room. The grandmother looked at me and said, "The poor kid, so much misfortune, and she is so young." Of the hundreds of people who had crossed their threshold to be helped to safety over the border, most were adults, some with children, but I was the first child to come alone. In spite of our awkward first encounter, they took a special interest in me.

Eventually the café emptied and the owners retired to the kitchen to eat their meal. Then they told me how I would cross the border that afternoon.

The railroad divided the village into two zones, the occupied on one side, the unoccupied on the other. Thus the village was a logical place to cross. The tracks marked the border. Most of the residents held passes that allowed them to move freely from one zone to the other, either to go to work or to visit relatives. The sentries knew these regulars well.

The railroad tracks were heavily and continually patrolled by armed soldiers who were well aware of the many who tried to cross illegally every day: Jews hoping to escape imprisonment; Gentiles crossing for political reasons; young men fleeing to escape mobilization or to join the Free French army in Africa or England.

My friends at the café were obviously *maquis* (members of the civilian *Résistance*), who helped many to safety. I am to this day filled with joy and thanks that "my" family was never discovered.

They had perfected their strategy of moving people across, until it was a science. They had to weigh many factors daily to maintain their level of success. The German guards changed their tactics at the drop of a hat to fool those who tried to cross illegally. They arranged erratic train schedules to destroy escapees' plans, and they devised other hazards to make the crossers' job more difficult. Obviously, the work of the café family involved many other people. These men and women often involved even their own children and went to any length to perform their underground duties.

Crossing the border was risky and could take place, of course, only when no train was expected. Two German guards patrolled the area, starting at opposite points. The guards walked toward each other until they met in the middle, where they did an about-face and walked away from each other. The crucial point occurred some meters before they reached their starting points and were about to turn and face each other again. At that point, the escapee would run across undetected, it was hoped, to safety.

The café owner's older daughter was assigned to help me cross, probably because it was thought that two young girls walking toward the railroad tracks would not attract too much attention. We had sent my meager luggage ahead to my cousins' home by railroad, so I had only an overnight bag, and we had sewn most of my money inside my jacket.

The young girl and I walked through the village. We had been told to act naturally, to chatter cheerfully as two girls of our age normally would. At first I was not afraid; all I could think of was that soon I would be safe and free with Josette. I would not have to be labeled any longer with a star. I would never fear arrest again.

Being painfully shy, I was at first anxious about staying with distant relatives, but I had no alternative. It would be best for Josette, and she was my foremost concern. As we neared the tracks, my self-assurance diminished considerably. From a distance I could see the heavily guarded barracks, similar in appearance to those at the borders.

It was nearly sundown when my companion took me to a spot near some dense brush bordering the tracks. She told me to stay low, to be quiet, and to run across as soon as she signaled me. She would be waiting for me in free France at her aunt's house, which we could see from our hiding place. I could see the guards' feet and legs through the branches when they met in the middle of the tracks right in front of us and stopped to exchange a few words. I was paralyzed with fear and sure that I would not be able to move, let alone run. My legs, which felt like two logs, would never carry me. My companion reassured me and finally tapped me on the shoulder and whispered, "Go! And don't stop running until you reach the other side. Run behind the low trees and into the ditch beside the road." I got up and ran faster than I had ever run in my life. Blindly I ran, until I tumbled headlong into the ditch. I was afraid to get up and walk on the road as she had instructed me, so I remained in the ditch for a long time. My feet were wet, my legs were spattered with mud, and I was shivering, but most of all I was terrified. I couldn't believe that I was in free France. It had happened so fast. I could hear the footsteps of the soldiers coming nearer. They'd see me! They'd shoot! When the soldiers met, they stopped right on the road above me and again exchanged words. This added to my fear.

It was night when I finally found enough courage to leave my hiding place and walk toward the lighted farm. My young friend had grown so nervous waiting at her aunt's house that she had started to walk to meet me. It was only when I neared the house that I really believed I was safe. I suppose that because of my youth I inspired a lot of compassion in most people, because I was greeted by the usual *"Oh, la, la! La pauvre gosse; elle est si jeune."* My friend stayed for a while and then went home to reassure her parents that all had gone well and that both of us were safe. She promised to return the next day to say good-bye. Her aunt and family were sympathetic and quite saddened by the tales that I told, at their insistence. I was so glad to be in free France that I didn't want to think of my unpleasant recent past.

In those days, and perhaps today, farmers lived with one set of in-laws. There was always a *mémé* (grandma) and, in some fortunate families, a *pépé* (grandpa). This home was no exception, and the *mémé* took a particular liking to me. After a generous meal, she sat by the fireplace to say a rosary for my parents' safety. I recall my room vaguely. I was most impressed by its extreme cleanliness, but I do recall how good it felt when I first lay down on the bed. The sheet was sun-dried and smelled sweet; the mattress felt so comfortable, and the down quilt was light and yet so warm.

The next morning when I woke up, my young friend was already there. The family gave me breakfast, and my friend told me that a car was waiting at the gas station to take passengers to the closest railroad station in Bourg-en-Bresse. She had made a reservation for me. I said my good-byes to the kind family and walked with my new friend toward the station. When we arrived, the driver told us the car was filled. This infuriated my companion, who insisted that she had reserved a seat for me on her way in. The driver denied this vehemently. The logical explanation for his denial is that he owned the only car making a round trip to the nearest large town, and someone must have paid a premium for my seat. I could have waited for the next trip, but I was eager to get started on my journey to the south of France. I had a long train ride ahead of me to Orange, about five hundred miles. So I decided to walk to Bourg-en-Bresse, against my friend's advice. I didn't trust the driver and suspected that I wouldn't have a seat for his next trip either.

I started on my journey, taking a narrow road through a dense forest in the Jura Mountains. After several hours of walking I was exhausted and afraid. Since I had started walking, I had not met a living soul. The quiet of the woods seemed as threatening as a houseful of Germans.

In a clearing I came upon a house and asked for shelter. The farmer was working the field, and his wife and her young children were quite surprised to see me. The sight of a young girl traveling on foot and alone through the forest was not an everyday occurrence. At another time, anyone who heard my story would have doubted it, but those were hard times, and anything was possible. This long walk was more than I had bargained for: my feet hurt, my stomach growled, and I was grateful when the woman asked me in. She suggested that I stay until the next day, when her uncle and his son would stop by on their weekly trip to Bourg-en-Bresse for provisions. They would give me a ride. I accepted the kind invitation and remained overnight. They were concerned about my welfare and made me promise to write as soon as I reached my family. (I corresponded with them for some time. When I went to boarding school later that year, they sent me several packages of food after I mentioned in one of my letters that I was hungry.)

The following morning I left with the uncle as planned, and in Bourg-en-Bresse I boarded a train bound for Lyons, where I caught another going to Orange. It was a long trip, and I arrived the next morning, exhausted, in Orange. There I would board a local to Bollène.

The train to Bollène did not leave for several hours, so I decided to go to the house Papa had lived in. I asked directions, and, as I walked through the town, I was impressed by its beauty. The architecture was different from that in my own part of France, with more colorful houses. The city was bathed in warm, bright sunshine almost year round. I came across many Roman ruins and, right in the middle of town, a most beautiful ancient amphitheater, which was still in use for opera, ballet, and plays. (To my delight, some time later the Rosembergs took the children and me there to see a presentation of *The Damnation of Faust*. It was an experience I never forgot: the night was warm and beautiful, and all the stars were out; the audience was responsive as only a European audience can be. I was mesmerized.)

The house Papa had lived in was on the main commercial street. On the street level was a store with two floors above it, where we would have lived. I spent a long and difficult few minutes there in front of the building, knowing what could have been but never would be. I wondered what my parents were doing at this time and felt almost guilty because I was free, standing there. Behind those doors were some of my parents' belongings and things that Tante Cecile and Uncle Albert had left behind. I tried the handle on the store door, but it was locked. A storekeeper from nearby noticed me and asked if I was looking for the owner. I was not about to confide in him, so I said simply, "Yes." He replied, "Oh, the Jew. He went back to the occupied zone to see his sick wife. It's been two months and he has not returned. The Germans probably caught him at the border." I thanked him and I walked back to the train station, crying all the way.

I had no idea what awaited me in Bollène. I walked for a long time until I saw a sign indicating that the house was at the end of a long tree-lined road. The house, le Château de Gourdon, was a castle in the middle of the Rosembergs' estate, where the family grew olives and peaches in addition to the principal crop, grapes, which were made into a good wine named after the castle. The Rosembergs employed several farmers and a manager who oversaw the whole operation. I was so impressed; I had never been inside an inhabited castle. I was a little intimidated, suffering from the beginning of what eventually developed into an acute inferiority complex. I was reluctant to ring the doorbell, though I knew the Rosembergs were expecting me, because Maman Marie had written to them.

I received a warm reception from Marceline, who was one month my senior and to whom I had been quite close in Epinal. Although we had once lived on the same street and attended the same school, I hardly knew the rest of her family, so her presence made my arrival among otherwise distant relatives quite pleasant. She was warm and happy to see me. I immediately inquired about Josette, and Marceline told me I would go to Limoges to fetch her as soon as we heard she had arrived. (Fortunately, the Rosembergs had a phone, a luxury in wartime.)

My cousin and her husband had five children, ranging in age from five to twenty-three. Henriette was married and lived in Orange; Henri, Marceline, Jacqueline, and little Michel were at home. I was to share Marceline's room, and Josette would stay in the nursery adjacent to the parents' room. Actually, I would have liked to share a room with Josette, but I didn't dare ask. For some reason, my cousins never told me how to address them, so I called them Mr. and Mrs. Rosemberg. Eventually, Mrs.

Rosemberg asked me to call her *ma cousine*, but I never could bring myself to do so, probably because I was intimidated by the family's position. The house was beautiful, its twenty-four rooms tastefully decorated, mostly with antiques, except the den, which would be described today as art deco.

Mrs. Rosemberg was an impressive and accomplished woman, like Maman, and a good businesswoman. She kept a tight rein on her five children and seemed to me authoritative and strict. Marceline, a middle child lost in the shuffle, and I became inseparable, and this made my life at their home bearable. But I suffered because of my extreme shyness, and I never spoke to the adults unless they addressed me directly.

When the Gertlers called to say that Josette had arrived in Limoges, I left to fetch her. I had never traveled so much in my life, and all alone. It was a long trip back to Lyons, across the center of France, and on to Limoges, where I found a distressed Josette, who had not stopped crying since she arrived. The exhausted Gertlers were relieved to see me. Josette had overheard someone say that I could be shot crossing the border; when I was not there to greet her, she was convinced that I was dead.

Mr. Gertler told me that the Red Cross was evacuating Jewish children to the United States, and he encourged me to apply for transport. He convinced me that it would be my parents' wish, that when the war was over either we could return to France or they could join us in the States. When he told me it was rumored that Jews were soon going to be arrested in the nonoccupied zone, I decided I must immediately go to Toulouse, to the Red Cross center. Mr. Gertler told me he had some business in Toulouse and would accompany Josette and me. Coincidentally, Mr. Aspis, the man to whom I had brought food daily in the prisoner of war camp until he escaped, had joined his family in Toulouse, and Mr. Gertler, who knew him, was sure that they would be only too happy to house us for a few days.

The Aspis family did take us in. Mr. Aspis spoke with overwhelming gratitude about my visits to him.

Josette and I went to the Red Cross center, and I filled out all the forms required. I was told that they would notify me of a date of departure at the address in Bollène. They were trying to gather the children who were hiding throughout unoccupied France with families or in convents.

We stayed only two or three days with the Aspis family. I was glad to leave because Mrs. Aspis treated us not badly but without feeling. The day we left for Bollène, she took us to the station, and I remember that she asked me if I had any money. When I said I did, she asked me to pay for our tickets. The Aspises were quite well-to-do, and I never forgot how hurt I was by this pettiness. (Many years later, when my son was three years old, I returned to France and visited the Aspises in their sumptuous store in Epinal. Mr. Aspis again spoke of his undying gratitude to me, but we were not asked to dinner or even for coffee at their home. I couldn't help comparing this to the hospitality of Maman Marie, who housed us all the time we were in Epinal.)

Josette adapted very well to life in the Rosemberg household and, in spite of her strong attachment to me, soon acquired a playmate in our cousin Michel, who was nine months older than she. Life would have been quite pleasant if only I had news from my parents. The cousins had many friends, young and old, who often came to visit; the house was never without guests. Still, I was often uncomfortable because I was the little cousin whose parents had been picked up by the Germans, the cousin who inspired more pity than friendliness from the many well-meaning visitors.

Tante Brigitte lived with her family in a small town near Vichy and came to Château de Gourdon often to visit her cousin. She always left her children with my uncle, claiming that she needed a rest. Well-meaning Tante Brigitte kept repeating that she had begged Maman to leave Epinal, but Maman would not listen. She implied that both Papa and Maman would be here if Maman had not been so stubborn. She seemed to have no compassion at all for my parents or for Josette and me. By convincing herself that Maman was solely responsible for her fate, Brigitte eased her own conscience. But how deeply her remarks hurt me! She repeated them to everyone who cared to listen. I wanted to scream, but, as I had been raised to be a young lady, I cried in my room instead. Needless to say, I didn't look forward to her frequent visits, and I welcomed her departures.

Tante Brigitte was a well-educated woman, fluent in several languages. It is amazing how some people can rationalize a situation they cannot or will not cope with, can actually convince themselves that they are in the right, and then can walk away with a clear conscience. It has always been my opinion that my aunt Brigette should have taken us in, rather than my Rosemberg cousins, who had five children of their own. She and Maman had been close, and Tante Brigitte was not exactly poverty stricken, but, on her frequent visits to Château de Gourdon, she never mentioned the possibility. Mr. Rosemberg brought up this point in front of me on several occasions, which certainly added to my growing inferiority complex.

Rumors that Jews were not as safe as they thought kept coming up in conversations among the adults, but no one seemed overly concerned. Life at Château de Gourdon was normal, food was plentiful, and the household was always lively. My young cousins had many friends in Bollène, most of them refugees from the occupied zone. They came to the house almost daily and gathered in the den. These young people lived *la dolce vita:* they had money and beautiful clothes, and they were concerned only with having fun. Most important, they had parents. For me, these get-togethers were pure hell. I couldn't feel at home; I would join the young people in the den, but often I would retire to my room to write to the many people I had befriended so recently. At that time their letters to me were the only source of comfort and hope in my otherwise unhappy life.

The Rosembergs were kind enough, and I was grateful that they took an interest in us. Mrs. Rosemberg took a particular liking to me, perhaps because I was always obedient, untroublesome, and willing to help around the house. So, instead of calling on one of her children when she needed something, she would call on me. Because this brought me at least some attention, I would run to her like a puppy.

Mr. Rosemberg was a kind, quiet man and seemed detached from most of the activities in the house. Until the German invasion in 1940, he had always been a businessman, and Château de Gourdon was just a summer home headed by a manager who took care of the estate. Mr. Rosemberg and Henri, the eldest son, had started to take an interest in the estate to busy themselves. Mr. Rosemberg adored his little son Michel. Though he rarely spoke directly to me—or perhaps I was too shy to speak to him—I have only fond memories of him.

Another frequent visitor to the Rosemberg home was my Uncle Leon, Maman's brother. He had visited us in

Epinal once or twice a year and would usually stay with Tante Cecile, his favorite sister. Uncle Leon had never married and had no special liking for children. Josette and I were no exception. He and Mrs. Rosemberg were fond of each other; therefore, he came often and would stay for long periods at a time. He was from the city of Lille in northern France and had settled in Pau in the Pyrenees near the Spanish border. He was a jeweler and an impeccably dressed ladies' man. During his visits he pretty much ignored Josette and me, speaking to me only to criticize. On one occasion my young cousins gave a party during which a guest invited me to dance. My uncle looked at me reproachfully and later on took me aside to tell me that he was thoroughly ashamed of my conduct. How could anyone dance when her parents were suffering in jail? Needless to say, his cruel words stung. It had been only about three months since my parents were taken away. Little did Uncle Leon know how painful it was for me to mix with happy young people when my heart was aching. I joined in party fun only at the insistence of Mrs. Rosemberg, who often found me sitting alone on the terrace when there were gatherings at the house. How did Uncle Leon know what I felt in my heart and how much I missed my parents? I wanted so much to be like everyone else, but I felt like a traitor whenever I enjoyed myself.

At Mrs. Rosemberg's urging, I visited Uncle Leon in Pau. It was a most uncomfortable few days for me: he criticized my every move, my looks, my attitude, even my clothing. But I was glad I went, because I was able to see the beautiful city of Pau. I saw Uncle Leon only twice after that visit. A year or so after we arrived in the States, he died of a heart attack. (Twenty-five years later Josette and I received Maman's meager share of his estate. Leon's girl friend of many years had squandered his fortune, but we did receive seven gold coins and two hundred dollars each. I wanted to have rings made out of the coins for my son, daughter, and husband for their birthdays. Someone recommended a young jeweler whose shop was nearby. My daughter Michele accompanied me to the store several times and there met and fell in love with the jeweler's younger brother, Joshua, whom she later married. I feel that in a strange way, Uncle Leon brought us happiness after all.)

The Rosembergs felt safe in Bollène. Perhaps they had paid someone to warn them in case of impending arrest. They were afraid to travel, however, and never left Château de Gourdon, except once, when Mr. Rosemberg took me to Orange to gather my parents' belongings. It was so painful to know that my parents, Josette, and I could have been living in that house at that very moment—if we had only left Epinal a day earlier. I recognized many or our things, but it was only when I found Papa's banjo that I realized the multitude of buts and ifs in my own life.

We took to Gourdon the valuables that my cousins promised to safeguard for us. The family asked me to turn the house over to Henriette, who badly needed an apartment. Spare furniture I left behind. As much as I loved Henriette, I hated to visit her in that house, which was literally furnished with my memories.

The Rosembergs decided that Marceline and I should resume our schooling. Since we had become inseparable, her parents insisted that for the good of our studies we should attend different schools. Marceline went to the *collège* in Orange, and I was sent to the *lycée des jeunes filles* in Avignon. Josette and I cried when I had to leave her, but she was happy with the Rosembergs and got along famously with Michel. I knew she was in good hands and that I would visit every other weekend, but still I left reluctantly.

My cousins had made arrangements for me to attend the *lycée,* and I went to Avignon unescorted. The school was even larger than the one in Dôle. It slightly resembled the Louvre in Paris and was perhaps a little severe in appearance but beautiful nevertheless. From its windows one could view the famous ruins of the pont d'Avignon and in the background, on a hill, the castle many Popes had called home.

I had always shared Papa's love of beauty, and Avignon provided many pleasant surprises. Walking through the streets that first day on my way to the school, I drank in the charming sites before me; I forgot for a while how nervous I was about starting in a new environment and arriving there alone. The southeast of France is rich in Roman relics, some extremely well preserved. Avignon has its share—the walls around the city and several beautiful arches, among other things. I rather enjoyed the long walk to school and wished it took longer.

Schools officially opened on October first, after the summer holidays, but I started late, in early November of 1942. When I arrived, I was introduced to the principal, who asked me a few questions before turning me over to a *surveillante,* who was in charge of watching the students between classes. She showed me around the school and eventually took me to the dormitory. The school was a converted convent, I think, because I recall a beautiful chapel in the yard.

Because my studies had been disrupted in the last year, my grades were low, and I had to have tutors in most of my subjects. Fortunately, this kept me busy, so I had little time to feel sorry for myself. But when I went to bed, I cried and wondered what had happened to my parents.

People in southern France are warm and friendly, and I

soon made some friends among the other boarders. Food was far from plentiful, and we were often hungry. I mentioned this in a letter to the café family who had sheltered me on my way to Bourg-en-Bresse, and they sent me several "CARE" packages in the months that followed. I never told my cousins that I was nearly starving, and they never asked me or even noticed that I had lost a great deal of weight. I went to the château on alternate weekends, as planned, and Josette always accompanied whoever came to pick me up at the station.

The French army had requisitioned most cars, and those that remained were in storage for lack of fuel. Certain people had permission to drive, of course, but cars were never used for pleasure. The Rosembergs' traveled in a horse-drawn carriage to Bolléne, where they bought their household provisions. It was this conveyance that picked me up at the station. I was always received well when I returned to Gourdon, and I was happy to see Josette and Marceline. If only my parents had been with us, life would have been quite pleasant for me.

But the news that the Germans were arresting Jews all over unoccupied France had reached Gourdon. One weekend when I returned to the château, an envelope from Maman Marie awaited me. It contained a letter from Papa:

Sept. 9, 1942

My very dear child,

I am writing these few words while riding with your mother in a cattle car, at full speed. There are fifty people per car: men, women, and children. We do not know our destination; we just passed EPERNAY, and it is rumored that they are taking us to POLAND. Meanwhile we are saying, "Good-bye to la belle

France." What they are going to do with us no one knows. Maybe it won't last long and we will see each other again. My dearest child, you must not forget your unfortunate parents, who have worked so hard in their youth and are leaving France this very moment without a cent, and with hardly any food to sustain themselves. Remember I wrote to you on several occasions, and asked you to send us packages and the money, but you never sent anything. Even the last day when we knew we would be deported we hoped you would. But it does not matter. I only want you to be reasonable from this day on. You must act like an adult and do what I tell you.

[He then instructed me where most of our valuables were hidden and with whom.]

Most of all do not give anything to anyone; keep everything yourself. Try to survive and to economize for us; you never know, perhaps one day we will return. Do not forget to take care of your little sister, Josette. Do not try to send us any packages; we won't be there. Give our regards to everyone and when the occasion arises you should go to the United States.

A thousand kisses,
Your father, Paul

My father had thrown this letter out of the cattle car, and a girl minding her cows nearby had found it. It was barely legible and so reached the Collinses many months later. It is still in my possession thirty-seven years later. I was able to recover very few of the valuables listed in the letter. As I mentioned earlier, most of the people Papa mentioned denied having anything of ours.

It was impossible for anyone to console me after I read that letter. My parents thought that I had deserted them! I was suffocating in guilt, in spite of the Rosembergs' repeated assurances that I had done what was asked of me, that the unscrupulous persons my parents had mentioned in their letters had stolen everything we sent. All I could think of was that they left believing I had failed them. This thought haunted me for years. When I finally accepted the fact that they were never coming back, I still wondered if they died thinking I could have saved them.

The Rosembergs kept me home for a week, but finally I went back to Avignon feeling worse than ever and wondering if I would ever see my parents again. I could not confide in anyone, which made it more difficult, because no one in school knew I was Jewish (I continued to be known as Jacqueline Glicen); as far as they knew, I lived in Bollène with my parents.

A few months went by. I never heard from the Red Cross; since Josette and I were being harbored, we were apparently not a priority case. At the news that the Germans were encroaching on the unoccupied zone and arresting Jews in large cities, Mrs. Rosemberg gave each of us children a small sack of money to wear on a string around our necks under our clothing in case we were separated. Soon we would have to leave Gourdon and disperse. It was late spring of 1943.

When I returned home one weekend, no one was at the station to pick me up. I walked toward Gourdon, more than a little concerned. As I approached the castle, I noticed German trucks on the road leading to the main house. Oh, my God! I didn't dare go farther but ran instead to the nearest farmhouse, where I learned that the Germans had taken away everyone in the house, including Marie and Susan, frequent visitors. Marie was engaged to my cousin Henri, who had left several months before to join Charles de Gaulle's Free French army.

All I could think of was that they had taken Josette. What was I to do now? I had failed my parents completely! I should have stayed with Josette. The farmers kept me overnight but suggested that I go to my nearest relative as soon as possible. With Germans swarming all over the place, I was not safe at their home.

My whole world was shattered. My parents had been deported to God only knew where. Now Josette and the whole Rosemberg family were gone. The only likely relative to go to was Tante Brigitte. She and her family lived in a village near Vichy called Saint-Pourcain. Fortunately, I had some money in the sack hanging around my neck. I left the next day and made the farmers promise they would write if they heard any news from Josette and the family. All I had were the clothes on my back and the overnight bag I had brought from school for the weekend at Gourdon.

I cannot say that Tante Brigitte received me with open arms. She was distraught at the news that her cousins had been arrested, because their arrest reinforced her fears for the safety of her own family. One more relative would only complicate matters.

Many people, not just Jews, had escaped from the occupied zone. Some were political refugees whose lives were in just as much danger. Therefore, housing in the unoccupied zone was at a premium, and one took anything that was available. My aunt and her family lived in a three-room apartment, small quarters for a family of five, and quite a contrast to the life-style to which Tante Brigitte was accustomed. Of all the married sisters, she pampered herself most, and the others often teased her about it. She was the only one who had not worked outside the home, and even there her maid had been in complete charge. Because she had been sickly as a child, her parents and later her husband spoiled her. It was perhaps harder for her to face adversity. She became nervous and was forever fighting with my uncle. In a small apartment, without domestic help, my poor cousin Ida became the head of the household as far as cooking and cleaning were concerned. Tante Brigitte was ill most of the time—psychosomatic illnesses, we thought—and she became quite helpless, finding strength enough only to argue with her husband. (They were divorced after the war.)

I was fifteen, disoriented, and burdened with sorrow. Like any teenager, I needed a strong adult. The confusion in that household did not help or encourage me in the least. Everywhere I turned there seemed to be darkness. I was happy only during the time I spent with my cousins Ida and Jeannine.

For some forgotten reason, I went to Vichy one day, perhaps to escape my unhappy surroundings for a while. Walking past a sidewalk café, I noticed a man who looked familiar, although I could not remember his name. I realized he was one of Papa's acquaintances from Epinal. Throwing caution to the wind, I introduced myself. He invited me home to meet his wife and children. I spent the afternoon with those good people, who were quite distressed by my tale. I cannot recall his name, but he played an important part in my life. I will refer to him as Mr. Maurice.

As daylight waned, Mr. Maurice offered to escort me home. He wanted to visit my aunt and uncle, whom he knew quite well. So he returned to Saint-Pourcain with me. My aunt and uncle were happy to see a familiar face, and they spent many hours talking about the good old days. I don't know what they said about me, but Mr. Maurice suggested that I return to Vichy with him, and he would take me to some farmers he knew well. There he said I would be safe and well taken care of. Tante Brigitte agreed and remarked that perhaps when I was settled she and her family could join me. It might be a haven for all of us. I was so unhappy at my aunt's, and Mr. Maurice inspired so much confidence, that I agreed. I welcomed any change; my only sorrow was that I had to leave my dear cousins behind. Tante Brigitte made me promise to write, and I left with Mr. Maurice the next morning. I spent the next two days at their home in Vichy and then left with him for Saint-Bonnet where his farmer friends lived.

We had to take several buses to our destination, but we finally arrived in Saint-Bonnet-d'Orcival, the smallest village I had ever seen, some thirty kilometers from Clermont-Ferrand. The village contained approximately twenty farms, a church, and a café that doubled as a grocery store. Built on a steep hill, the village was scarcely noticeable from the main road, making it a rather good hiding place. The countryside was lovely; the farm I was to live on was at the bottom of the village near a small stream. Somehow I felt safe in this remote place. When we reached the house, Mr. Maurice asked me to remain outside. He wanted to speak to the farmer alone.

After some time Mr. Maurice finally called me in and introduced me to the Lassalas family. Farmers in that part of the country spoke a patois that I eventually understood well but always spoke haltingly. The family consisted of La Mémé, a widow; her son Baptiste; his wife Jeanne; their child Ririe; and a half-brother simply called Lassalas.

[79]

In France in those years the *paysans* (peasants) were a breed apart. They lived in almost the same conditions as had their parents and grandparents before them, and they kept the old traditions. Only the wealthy farmers could send their children to large cities for schooling. In most cases those same parents later regretted their choice of schools when their offspring refused to return to their native villages and take over their responsibilities at the farms.

Only peasants in the soil-poor regions would abandon their villages to seek employment in large cities. The majority of them went to Paris, which, even the French regarded as heaven on earth. Some made it; many didn't but were too ashamed to return home and thereby admit failure. Many a song has been written about the peasant girl who went to Paris to seek her fortune only to end up a lady of the night.

The Lassalas were typical country people of the Puy de Dôme region. Their life-style was alien to me. When I first entered the room that served as kitchen, dining room, and family room, I was met by every member of the family. All of them looked at me with curiosity, even Jeanne, who also gave me a big and friendly smile. La Mémé was obviously the head of and spokesperson for the household. My first impression of her was that she would be a stern and forbidding foster parent. I was wrong. In spite of her humble background—she could barely read or write and had never left her village in her sixty years—La Mémé was as queenly in her bearing as any monarch. She looked me over carefully and finally said, "*La petite*, we will take you in on one condition: we never have had in our home anyone who did not go to church. I believe it is bad luck. No one in the village is to know you are Jewish because we don't want to get shot by the Germans." La Mémé was quite a beautiful woman. Like most older French women of the period, she always wore black: once in mourning, always in mourning. At first she was severe, even authoritarian toward me, but as time went by, she soon revealed to me the proverbial heart of gold.

Mr. Maurice stayed to gather some provisions for his family and promised to come back the following week. When he left, I suddenly realized that I was going to live on a farm with complete strangers who spoke a language foreign to me and who at the moment were making no attempt to help me feel at home. Most of them left the family room to resume their activities, while I remained there with La Mémé (pronounced May May) and little Ririe, who was about four. The sight of Ririe reminded me of Josette, and I started to cry. Instead of putting her arms around me to soothe me, La Mémé tried to divert me by asking questions about my background. At the sight of my scanty belongings, all contained in an overnight bag, she concluded the obvious: I didn't have a wardrobe suitable for the country—or the city, for that matter. She decided we would have to make some clothes for me. Meanwhile, I could have some of Jeanne's, as she was about my size. La Mémé's voice was of an even tone and showed no emotion, but her interest in me showed kindness and made me feel more at ease.

Most farms in the village consisted of a large barn where the farmers kept the hay; the stables, which always included a bedroom in one corner; the traditional large kitchen–family room; and perhaps another bedroom. The room in the stable was simply a space enclosed with barbed wire. It was considered top choice in the winter because, with all the cattle nearby, it was very warm.

The inside of the Lassalas house was, by comparison,

quite luxurious and attractive: each of its seven or eight rooms was charmingly decorated with plain old country furniture now considered antique. I recall vividly the beautiful armoires in the bedrooms. The main room, the center of all activities, was quite large and comfortable and probably looked exactly as it had several generations before. The walls were old brick, and as one entered one faced a large fireplace where La Mémé actually did the cooking for the family. She baked bread once a week in a small brick bake house that contained two large community ovens. There was no indoor plumbing: the outhouse stood at the far end of the garden, and the family brought water into the house from a fountain some five hundred feet away.

La Mémé was in complete control of all activities in and around the farmhouse. Each morning, like a general, she solemnly recited to each household member his or her duties for the day. She commanded and received the greatest respect.

Little Ririe was very attached to her grandmother and even shared her bedroom. She really was raised by her grandmother, while Jeanne was busy tending to her outdoor duties. Jeanne worked hard, without ever complaining. She rose at dawn to milk the cows with Lassalas and continued with her chores until sundown. Even though she was known around the village for having stamina equal to that of many men, Jeanne was the most charmingly feminine, pleasant, and kind individual one could ever meet. She became my friend almost immediately. Her husband Baptiste was a typical Auvergnat (a person from the region of Auvergne) and, like most, was taciturn. I was ill at ease in the presence of Baptiste for a long time, but he eventually warmed toward me and showed a genuine concern for my welfare. He took his responsibilities toward me so seriously that he acted at times as if he were my father. When the young men in the village flirted with me, Baptiste quickly discouraged them. I always remained a little afraid of him and was shy when I had to address him. Baptiste was a superb artisan; from his shop, which was attached to the main house, came beautifully crafted country furniture. Because of his work, Baptiste rarely performed duties around the farm. The chores were left solely to Jeanne and Lassalas.

On that first day I was not shown my room until late in the evening. I was pleasantly surprised. People today pay large amounts of money to decorators to achieve the provincial effect that the Lassalas family took for granted. Jeanne said this would be my private domain. My room was large and, in keeping with the rest of the house, spotless. Among its furnishings was an elaborately carved traditional armoire, a water pitcher and bowl, and (discreetly placed in a corner) a covered pail, a necessity in case one could not wait for the morning's trip to the outhouse. The floor was stained dark and was covered only by a throw rug near the brass bed. In addition, there were a table and four chairs and an exquisitely enameled wood-burning stove. Beauty in simplicity. Even in such comfortable quarters, however, I cried myself to sleep and felt guilty to be so lucky. My parents were suffering God only knew what tortures, and my little Josette was missing.

Jeanne woke me early the next morning to join the family at breakfast, and I knew I looked painfully shy when I entered the main room. Jeanne tried hard to make me feel at ease, and La Mémé decided, since we got along so well, that I would help her with her daily chores around the farm. I must admit that I never became adept at them, and the others often teased me about my city ways. I tried hard, though, and they appreciated my efforts.

On the first Sunday I spent with the family, La Mémé went to early Mass, as she always did; Jeanne, Ririe, and I went to the eleven o'clock service. I was no stranger to the Mass; I had attended many times with our housekeeper and had visited beautiful churches and cathedrals with Papa. But this was the first Sunday I *had* to go to church. Jeanne gave me clean clothes to wear, and we all left the house in our Sunday best. I felt conspicuous when I entered the church that first time, since everyone stared at me and wondered who was this new addition to the Lassalas family.

Mass was, of course, still said in Latin then, and the church was poorly lighted, which added a certain mystery to the ritual. Although I was familiar with churches, I certainly didn't understand the many parts of the Mass, so I felt awkward. But soon I learned to sit, stand, and kneel only a split second after everyone else did. Occasionally, during that first obligatory Mass, Jeanne would look up and smile, as if to say, "You're doing well." I asked God to forgive me for masquerading and was relieved when it was time to leave and return to the farm where La Mémé had prepared a delicious Sunday dinner.

After the meal, La Mémé called me into her room and told me that I would have to go to confession, as everyone else in the family did. She didn't want to evoke any curiosity among the other parishioners. I hadn't bargained for that! When she noticed my reluctance, she simply said, "Don't worry, little one. You will do just fine." I don't think anyone can truly understand the chaotic thoughts that spun in my head. My parents had raised me to be truthful and honest. To me, a religious masquerade was

[84]

the ultimate hypocrisy, completely against Papa's teaching. I thought I'd be committing an act for which he could never fogive me, but I dared not argue with La Mémé.

Naturally, I was nervous the first time I went to confession. I recall mumbling a string of "misdemeanors": I lied once, I was greedy at supper, and so on. I had a terrible case of the shakes, and I was greatly relieved when Father gave me a penance of a few Our Fathers and Hail Marys, blessed me, and sent me on my way. Confession was a piece of cake, however, compared with my first Holy Communion. I was literally unable to swallow the host given to me by the priest and was absolutely sure that this inability was a sign from God: "Hey! *You* don't belong here!" I couldn't share this horrible certainty with anyone. I was shy and ashamed of my feeling, and it was too difficult to deal with my mixed emotions.

As time went on, however, I began to look forward to Sundays. I enjoyed Mass and Vespers, which we attended in late afternoon. Quiet prayer, the hymns, the droning of the priest: these soothed the troubled thoughts I lived with. I grew to like playing Catholic. It was safer than being Jewish. Jews had to pay such a high price for survival. Unfortunately, I started to think that perhaps Jews were bad; otherwise why would God allow anyone to persecute them? (I had not learned one Catholic belief: that God tests those he loves.) By then, actually, I was ashamed of my heritage. The Lassalas family had told curious villagers that my parents were political prisoners with communist inclinations who had been deported to a labor camp in Germany. Most known communists had been arrested, so such a story made sense.

About a month went by, and I still had no news about Josette. I wrote to the farmers in Gourdon, but they did not answer my letter. I felt a crushing pain every time I thought of her; otherwise, life would have been bearable. I worked hard at the farm, and the members of the Lassalas family, especially Jeanne, were kind in their own stern way and treated me as one of them. Around La Mémé and Baptiste, Jeanne was a little afraid to let her hair down, but she loved life. When we were alone in the fields, she made me laugh and told me tales about her youth and the villagers. I enjoyed being with her most of all. When I was depressed, she consoled me by telling me that the war would soon be over, that my parents would come back, that Josette was in good hands and was probably with somone who simply did not have my address and so could not write to me. She said that the Boches had to lose, because good always triumphed over evil. Her encouragement kept my heart and soul from shriveling with bitterness and despair.

One day as Jeanne and I came back from minding the cows, La Mémé handed me a letter addressed to me and postmarked in the city of Arles, in southern France. I knew no one in Arles; I had never even been there. The letter had been sent to Tante Brigitte, who had forwarded it to me in Saint-Bonnet. I was a little afraid to open it. It was from a lady who was taking care of Josette. She was a friend of the Rosembergs' maid, who had brought Josette to her.

I was crazy with joy! I could not believe it. The whole Lassalas household laughed and cried with me, and Jeanne kept saying, "You see, I was right." When I calmed down, I asked La Mémé if I could bring Josette back to stay with me at their home. She agreed wholeheartedly, but the family hesitated to let me travel alone and with my identification card; my name was unmistakably Jewish. Baptiste said I needed false papers. (I did not know it at the time, but he was a maquisart with the underground. I did not find out about his many contributions and courageous activities until the war was over.) He obtained for me, through one of his connections, papers bearing a false name, which he made sure I memorized. Two days later I left to fetch Josette.

It was a long journey from the station in Clermont-Ferrand to Arles. I still had some money left, and La Mémé gave me enough provisions for the round trip. The ride was uneventful. Unfortunately, I again had to come in close contact with many German soldiers. It had been a welcome relief not to see any in Saint-Bonnet, and I felt uneasy when the gestapo checked my papers on several occasions. I worried that in spite of my false identification they would ask my reason for traveling alone.

But I arrived safely in Arles and went straight to the house where Josette was staying. The woman was, of course, shocked to see me, for I had arrived without warning. Josette was in school, and, while we waited for her to return, the woman told me how my sister had been spared.

On that fateful morning Mrs. Rosemberg had taken Jacqueline, Michel, and Josette for a walk on the estate. When they returned, they noticed as they came closer to the main house that Germans were swarming all over the place. Mrs. Rosemberg ran with the children to her nearest neighbor, who took them away immediately to another house a distance from Gourdon, where they stayed overnight. Eventually they made it to Arles, where the maid came from and still had many relatives. Mrs. Rosemberg was in hiding nearby, and the children were with someone else, but Josette's protector refused to tell me where. Mr. Rosemberg, Marceline, Marie, and Suzanne, all of whom had remained in the house, had of course been arrested.

The woman said that because I was a mere child myself she could not entrust Josette to me. She had become very attached to her. The only other member of the household was her young daughter-in-law, whose husband was in a prisoner-of-war camp in Germany. The woman's own husband was in the hospital.

Josette finally came home from school, and we both cried at the sight of each other. Her blonde curly hair, her little upturned nose, and her blue eyes never looked more beautiful. More important, I was happy to see her alive and well. I think the woman was moved by our obvious love for each other, because she lost some of her stern demeanor. She asked me to remain for dinner and to spend the night. I shared the daughter-in-law's room, and we talked most of the night: she about the husband she missed so much, and I about my parents. She told me that Josette had become for her a symbol of innocence in a world filled with evil and unhappiness. Because she understood how much it meant for Josette and me to be together, however, she told me she would try to persuade the older woman to change her mind about allowing Josette to leave with me. I could have left Josette at their home, where she was well taken care of and loved, but I would not. She was my responsibility; my parents' last wishes were that I should take care of her.

The woman asked me to remain another day. She claimed she had to visit her husband in the hospital, but I have always suspected that she went to Mrs. Rosemberg for advice. In her absence, the younger woman took me on a tour of Arles, another old and historic city containing many interesting Roman ruins. I was impressed and enjoyed the day immensely, but I was anxious to confront the older woman. I had made up my mind that if she refused to let me take Josette, she would have to keep me as well. When we returned, she was impatiently waiting for us. She said she had given the matter a lot of thought and had decided that it was bad enough for us to be separated from our parents, that she had no right to keep us apart, too. We could leave the next day if I wished.

When I came downstairs the next morning, the older woman was gone. She couldn't bear to say good-bye to Josette. The younger woman took us to the train station, and we left, never to return to Arles. The train from Arles to Lyons was crowded with civilians. Josette was an engaging child who attracted everyone's attention and made some friends on the train.

I don't remember what imaginative answer I gave to the many inquisitive passengers. But I clearly recall that Josette, who must have been George Washington in another life, corrected me incessantly. I had a hard time keeping her quiet. It is not easy for a child of five to lie.

There was a layover of several hours in Lyons until we could catch a train to Clermont-Ferrand. To my dismay, an army convoy was the only train available. I was eager to get back, so I decided to take it in spite of my fears.

Meanwhile, Josette and I stayed in the crowded waiting room. We had to sit on the floor among the many other travelers. I took out some food, and, as I gave tidbits to Josette, I noticed an old man, who, judging from the look on his face, was quite hungry. I handed him a slice of salami meant for Josette, who exploded in a fit of anger. I couldn't calm her down. She kept saying, "We won't have any food. Why did you have to give it away?" The poor man had already taken a few bites and was absolutely stunned. It might have been comical if it hadn't been so pathetic. Josette already knew, at five, the meaning of being hungry, and, worse still, knew from bitter experience that only the strong survive.

I managed to calm Josette and assure the old man that we had sufficient food left for ourselves. He said, "God bless you."

We finally boarded our train, which was ninety-nine percent filled with German soldiers. In the open cars at the end of the train one could see heavy artillery. I tried in vain to find a compartment filled with civilians. I did spot an elderly couple sitting among some soldiers. Fortunately, there were two empty seats near them. Josette fell asleep shortly after the train began to move. In Saint-Etienne the couple who shared our compartment got off, and two soldiers who had been standing in the corridor took their seats. I didn't dare change compartments, so I closed my eyes and tried to sleep. I must have just dozed off when we were awakened by the screeching of the train's brakes. I soon heard shooting and saw German soldiers jumping off the train yelling, "Raus, raus." Both Josette and I were a bit foggy with sleep, but I grabbed her and ran. Many large Allied planes were flying overhead. German soldiers from the train were running toward the woods bordering the railroad tracks and kept yelling as they passed by, "Run!" I was carrying Josette, who was quite heavy, and I couldn't run up the steep incline to the forest. None of the soldiers passing me offered to help. By then, the gunfire was heavier, and the planes seemed to be almost on top of us. Josette screamed in terror. I begged the soldiers passing by to help me carry Josette up the hill. Since no one would, I held Josette against my body inside the heavy coat I was wearing, wrapped my arms around her, and threw myself on the ground, face down, on top of her. We remained there until the shooting and the noise of the planes subsided. I could hear the soldiers yelling and running in all directions, mostly toward the end of the train where most of the damage had taken place.

There was but a handful of civilians on the train, and the only casualties, to my knowledge, were some soldiers who had been guarding the artillery cars. I had witnessed bombings and shootings on several other occasions, but one just doesn't get used to this sort of danger. We were shaken, but glad to be alive. The soldiers ordered the few civilians to reboard the train, at gunpoint, and rounded us up into the same car. In spite of our misadventure we were glad that the Allies were at long last coming to our rescue, and we finally started to believe that perhaps we were going to be liberated. It was several hours before the damaged cars were removed from the tracks and the train started to move.

We arrived in Saint-Bonnet the next day and received a royal welcome. La Mémé kept saying she had had nightmares about our being killed and feared she would never see me alive again. Josette shared my room that night, and I felt really good for the first time since the day the Germans arrested our parents. I wrote to Maman Marie to tell her that Josette was with me. She and her family loved Josette so much; I knew they would want to know how she was.

Josette and little Ririe, not quite a year younger, became good friends, and soon Josette moved into La Mémé's room because Ririe refused to go to bed without her. All of us were glad that Ririe had a playmate. She was a shy little girl who rarely spoke to strangers. After several weeks, Ririe seemed to come out of her shell and grow more talkative. She and Josette were soon inseparable. Partly because of Ririe, Josette was happy to be with

me in her new surroundings. I felt more relief than anything else.

The farmers in various regions of France were the only
ones who managed to eat well. They even made some
money selling provisions to the many city dwellers who
swarmed the countryside every weekend in search of fresh
foods. The government had assessed every farm and had a
good idea of the total production of each. The Vichy ad-
ministration had requisitioned a certain percentage of
crops for the Nazis. There was no shortage of food in
Germany in those war years, but much of the population
in Nazi-occupied territory all over Europe was starving.

Somehow the farmers managed to produce enough to
satisfy the Nazis and still keep a surplus to feed themselves and to sell. For everything that it requisitioned the
government paid farmers a mere pittance. Farmers who
before the war had been taken for granted became quite
important to city dwellers. The Lassalas family made
their own cheese and salami and always had an abundance of eggs. Occasionally they would kill a pig or a
steer, and they bred rabbits, a French favorite.

Mr. Maurice came almost every week. It must have
warmed his heart to know that he was responsible for
finding such a wonderful family to look after us. I never
succeeded in becoming a farm girl, but in a small way I
was able to help the Lassalas family with the bookkeeping
and correspondence. For this they were grateful and even
became dependent on me. I was happy to contribute and
happier still to feel needed.

The highlight of our evenings was to listen to Radio
London, a forbidden acitivity, of course. The Germans
worked hard to create interference; at times we could
scarcely hear the transmission. Nevertheless, every night

at ten we would be glued to the radio in the hope of catching the encouraging messages for occupied France from the Free French stationed in England. Messages came from soliders to reassure their families that they were safe. We had news of the war in general. Later on I found out that Radio London also transmitted coded messages to the French underground.

At the end of the summer of 1943, Josette started classes in a charming, two-room school run by a husband and wife. Josette adapted well, and the teacher was happy with her and her progress.

It wasn't long before I became friendly with all the young people in the village, but it had been difficult to win them over. I was, after all, a city girl. Jeanne was responsible for breaking down the barriers. She had a long talk with some of the girls and insisted that they include me in their activities. At first, some were reluctant to accept me. They had known one another from birth and had gone to school together. Theirs was an exclusive sorority, but they grudgingly granted me admittance. The girls eventually became fond of me and were genuinely interested in my welfare. The activities in a small village are limited. The girls met in the fields while minding their cattle and attended an occasional dance in a barn on Sunday afternoons until it was time to go to Vespers in the early evening.

I soon had a best friend, Bernadette. She worked in an office in Clermont-Ferrand, where she lived with her widowed mother. They both came to visit her mother's sister on weekends and spent their month's vacation in Saint-Bonnet. She had grown up in the village and was close to the young people. She was at least four years older than I, but she took a special interest in Josette and me. Bernadette and her mother became quite fond of me and I of them. Each Friday I would wait impatiently for them at the bus stop.

I had a lovely singing voice as a child, and I was asked to join the church choir. On Christmas I had the privilege of singing a solo: "Minuit Crétien," which Jeanne teasingly accused me of jazzing up when I rehearsed at home.

Many farmers in Saint-Bonnet and the vicinity were prisoners of war. Before Christmas that year the young people of the village and surrounding isolated farms combined their efforts to raise money for them by performing in a variety show. We made costumes from things we borrowed from cooperative villagers. Baptiste rounded up some of the young men to help build a stage in an abandoned barn. We borrowed chairs and benches for the audience. Bernadette and I staged the complete performance, which included a play, solo singers, dances that we choreographed, and a comedian. Bernadette and I also performed in the play, and I sang two solos, one of which featured my self-taught yodeling. I don't remember how we advertised, but people came from miles around. With standing room only, the show was a huge financial success. We collected a lot of money, which we used to send packages to the POWs and to help their needy families. I like to think our show was an artistic success. I know I enjoyed it.

Recycling became an art. La Mémé would rip up old clothes and use the material to sew new ones for the entire family, which now included Josette and me. The family also raised sheep; La Mémé processed their wool and spun it on a foot-powered spinning wheel. La Mémé taught me to knit. She despised idleness, and during our spare time we would knit sweaters, socks, even underwear for the cold winters. In the evening while listening to Radio London one could hear the clicking of busy knitting needles in addition to the static of the broadcast.

Lassalas was Baptiste's half-brother. Their father must have been rather old when he married La Mémé, because Lassalas was almost as old as she was—or at least he appeared to be. For some reason Lassalas and Baptiste did not speak to each other; for that matter, La Mémé spoke to Lassalas only when it was absolutely necessary. Jeanne was the only one who communciated with him. Yet he took part in all the household activities, and his needs were attended to as quickly as anyone else's. I never questioned the reason. It seemed to me that Lassalas was a little simple, a condition that seemed not to bother him at all. He was jovial and spoke to everyone whether they answered him or not. Most of all, he enjoyed the children. He was a tall, slim, but extremely strong man and worked very hard on the land. Since he spoke mostly patois, he and I never formed any kind of relationship, but he always greeted me kindly and helped me when I needed him. He took all his meals with the family, but retired to his room in the barn.

Mr. Chaumette was the official mayor of Saint-Bonnet, actually the *adjoint*. (The vice-mayor took over most of his duties.) The Chaumettes resided in Clermont-Ferrand, and the mayor visited the village every other week or so until the summer, when he and his family, which included married children and grandchildren, occupied their castle.

I must have attracted his attention at some time, probably when he attended the show we put on for the POWs, because in the early summer of 1944 he came to the farm and told La Mémé that he would like to hire me for the two months or so that he and his family spent vacationing in their summer residence. Mr. Chaumette was a tall, handsome, distinguished, and soft-spoken man in his late sixties. He was well-respected by all the villagers. By then I had completely run out of money, and this seemed to be a good opportunity to earn some so that I could pay for our room and board.

The Chaumettes' castle did not look at all like my cousins' Château de Gourdon but more like the ones dating from the Middle Ages that were pictured in my history books. It was apparent from the architectural difference that a wing had been added sometime later. When I knocked at the front door for my interview with Mrs. Chaumette, I was told by a member of the family to come in through the service entrance. When Mrs. Chaumette, a handsome and polite—albeit reserved—woman, interviewed me, she spoke to me in the manner that French aristocrats were accustomed to using when they addressed their hired help, whom they regarded as inferior. The French were very class conscious in those days. Money did not open all doors; position and titles did, even if the bearers of those titles were poverty-stricken. I was intimidated by the house when I first saw it, and I was even more intimidated by Mrs. Chaumette. No one had ever spoken to me in such a condescending manner.

The house was enormous, with at least thirty rooms, all furnished with the most exquisite antiques, including priceless tapestries, paintings, and rugs. The formal living room was a sight to behold, with its many French windows (which I had to clean once a week) that opened on a balcony overlooking the beautiful countryside. The staff consisted of a cook, a laundress who came once a week, and now me. The household, headed by Mr. and Mrs. Chaumette, included their two unmarried children (a young man of about twenty-four and his sister, around twenty), two married daughters and their spouses, who were brothers and boasted the title of count. (We had to address them as Monsieur le Comte or Madame la Comtesse.) Six grandchildren completed the family. My duties were varied. I was hired as a *bonne à tout faire* (maid of all work), a title that Mrs. Chaumette interpreted literally, I was soon to discover.

Josette was reluctant to let me leave, and none of my arguments seemed to carry much weight. How was I to explain to this six-year-old child that I had to earn a living? She thought I was deserting her, and, as a result, Josette became hard to handle until I eventually reassured her that I would visit her briefly on Sundays. I was as reluctant to leave her behind as she was to have me go. I felt secure at the Lassalas farmhouse, and the prospect of being a maid didn't appeal to me in the least, but I had committed myself and was too shy to express my fears to La Mémé. Besides, I did need to earn money, and the job was only for the summer.

On my first day of work, Mrs. Chaumette informed me that I would have to address the members of the family in the third person. This was very difficult for me. For example, I couldn't say, "Would you like your breakfast served in bed, madame?" That would have been considered unpardonable. Instead I had to ask, "Does madame wish to have her breakfast in bed?" She corrected me many times daily for my mistakes. I dared to say, "Are you pleased, madame?" instead of "Is madame pleased?" I should have considered myself lucky that I didn't have to back out of rooms, as did some hired help.

When Mrs. Chaumette made her third-person stipulation, I was ready to return to the comfort of the Lassalas home. I do not intend to denigrate anyone who works as a housekeeper by saying that my parents did not raise me to be a maid or that I was too good for the job. But my parents certainly did raise me to have high standards, and they never expected me to be treated like a second-class citizen. A maid, to some French aristocrats, was just that. My parents and I had been subjected to discrimination by the Nazis, it is true, but even that was somehow more acceptable than discrimination at the hands of a French citizen, a countryman. Mrs. Chaumette treated me more as a convenient object than as a human being, and she had no regard for my feelings. I wanted to yell out to this pompous woman that I came from a home in which maids were treated as members of the family, by people as "good" as the Chaumette family, but I was too shy and too polite. Most important, I could not be disrespectful to an older person. No matter what I was thinking, I listened patiently to Mrs. Chaumette's humiliating demands.

When I was hired as a *bonne à tout faire*, I didn't realize how precisely Mrs. Chaumette would define my title. I rose each morning at six with Marie, the cook, a kind but rather deaf old woman. We were both allowed to retire around ten at night after we had thoroughly cleaned the kitchen. The sixteen hours in between were chockablock.

Marie started the fire in the wood-burning stove, using wood I had brought in the previous evening, while I busied myself setting the huge table in the dining room for breakfast for the fourteen members of the household. I served breakfast promptly at nine after changing into my daytime maid's uniform.

Besides my daily routine of serving meals and cleaning, I was also expected to amuse the children in the afternoon and to help them dress and undress. I cleaned bedrooms, made all the beds, and emptied the *seaux*, or chamber pots, which I washed and disinfected daily. (Although one bathroom served the household, some members were too lazy to walk that far during the night.)

Another task I abhorred was to *faire les couvertures* (uncover the beds) every night before the family retired to their quarters. I could not do this in just any manner. After removing and folding the bedspread, I had to fold back the bedclothes on each side just far enough for *madame et monsieur* to enter on their respective sides, but I had to leave an unfolded space in the middle. This carefully folded cover signified that these superior beings never touched each other after entering their bed. I was severely reprimanded when on several occasions I performed this task less than perfectly.

I helped Marie in the kitchen. I cleaned the huge French windows. I ironed, polished the silver, cleaned and vacuumed every room, and served breakfast, lunch, and dinner, of course.

The good life was over. I didn't dare tell the Lassalas family that I was going to hate every minute of my stay with the Chaumettes.

Thus I started my working life. The children of the household and eventually Marie, the old cook, were kind to me, but the others ordered me about and often scolded me sharply. The exception was Mr. Chaumette, who smiled often and occasionally mumbled a kind word to me—but never in anyone else's presence. I was free after breakfast on Sunday to go to Mass and, after I served lunch, I could spend a few hours with Josette, but I had to return in time to serve dinner. The Lassalas family soon realized I was miserable, although I never complained. Jeanne used to say that the summer would soon be over. Josette missed me a lot, and La Mémé complained that she cried for me. I saw her every Sunday and, if she finally got accustomed to my new life-style, *I* did not!

Each tremendous room of the Chaumettes' summer house was more beautiful than the other—except Marie's and mine, of course, which were in the attic, semi-finished and semi-furnished. My dimly lit room had only a mattress on the floor and a small dresser. I kept the light on all night, for it was my only company.

Mrs. Chaumette often questioned me about my parents. She seemed suspicious of my answers, but I stuck to my story: "The Germans picked up my parents as communists and put them in a labor camp." I do not know what she considered worse, being a Jew or being a communist. I think Mrs. Chaumette probably hated one as much as the other.

Mrs. Chaumette supervised her household with a sharp eye. She accounted for all provisions and kept them under lock and key in the large pantry adjoining the kitchen. She dictated the daily menus to the cook each evening and then presented her with the same menu in writing. Mrs. Chaumette rose early each morning to attend Mass in nearby Saint-Bonnet. On returning, she distributed the ingredients necessary to prepare whatever dishes she had ordered for that particular day—no less and no more than was needed. Marie grumbled every day that she had never worked under such strict supervision and that if she didn't need the money to survive, she would return without a moment's notice to her home in Clermont-Ferrand. Marie and I took our meals after the family, eating mostly whatever was left over. Mrs. Chaumette and Marie bickered continually over the preparation of the meals, and, since Marie was quite deaf, the large kitchen was usually filled with shouting. Marie had worked for many so-called better families and claimed she had never worked for anyone as stingy as Mrs. Chaumette, who had hired her for the summer and then asked her to continue on at their permanent residence in Clermont-Ferrand. Marie flatly refused this dubious honor and confided in me that this job was making her a nervous wreck. When we were hired, Marie and I had to submit our food-ration coupons to Mrs. Chaumette. She weighed our bread daily, which, I recall, infuriated the cook, especially in view of the fact that Mrs. Chaumette cheated a bit, and never in our favor. Marie never ate bread and always gave me her portion. When Mrs. Chaumette found this out, she was furious with Marie and took her ration away. The cook became so angry that she decided to quit and went up to her room to pack. It was quite amusing that day to watch the Chaumette women struggling to prepare the meals, fighting among themselves, and leaving the kitchen in such a mess that one would have thought they had cooked for an army. Somehow Mrs. Chaumette convinced Marie to remain until the end of the summer but gave her no bread ration again, and I now felt unworthy of my own piece of bread.

The rivalry between the two married Chaumette sisters was quite apparent. The older girl was the more attractive and was also the wealthier. Each, of course, had married into an illustrious French noble family. The older sister was definitely her mother's pet. The two sisters spoke to each other only to bicker. The younger girl was unquestionably homely and was very nasty to me. I disliked her intensely. The other was distant but kinder when she addressed me, until one day she returned to her room and noticed that I had forgotten to turn down the covers. She came into the kitchen where I was drying the supper dishes and reprimanded me so harshly that I finally broke down and cried out to her, while sobbing uncontrollably, "My mother and father were just as good as or better than you. It isn't the end of the world, and *you* aren't crippled. For once you can turn down your own blankets!" She was no more stunned than I. I had never before spoken to an adult in that manner. I was sure that this would be the end of my job at the Chaumettes', but when Mrs. Chaumette entered the room shortly thereafter, she simply asked me to apologize to Madame la Comtesse and made me promise to watch my tongue in the future. She was almost kind.

When I apologized to the countess, she told me I had lost a great opportunity, as she had intended to take me home with her to Lyons to care for her children. She told me that I was great with her children and that they loved me. Actually, I was quite fond of her children. They and Marie were my only friends in that household, and at least I didn't have to speak to the children in the third person.

At night in my bed, I often cried when I thought of my parents and of how upset they would be if they knew that I was a maid. Little did I know at the time how fortunate I was and how gladly my parents would have performed the duties of maid and butler for the Chaumettes.

It was summer, so I often kept the bedroom window open and read myself to sleep. Late one particularly warm night, a bat, attracted by the light, fluttered into my room. I covered my face with the sheets, but the bat kept flying all around me because the light was near my bed. I screamed hysterically. The first person to reach my room was the Chaumettes' unmarried son, quickly followed by his parents. They chased the bat out and reprimanded me for causing so much commotion and for disturbing the household in the middle of the night. They also scolded me for allowing their son to see me in my night clothes and for my worst crime—using electricity so carelessly. I hated going to my room even more from then on, and I never opened the window again.

I have not mentioned the younger Chaumette children for good reason: they never spoke to me in all the time I worked there until this incident occurred.

Maman Marie Collins wrote to me quite often to reassure me that France would soon be liberated and that when my parents came back they would be so proud of me. Although she was born a Catholic, Maman Marie never went to church. She claimed to be a Christian Scientist; I say "claimed" because, to my knowledge, she never went to any services. But she believed in the Christian Science doctrine, and she kept telling me that hell was on earth and that we had to be punished here to deserve the better life that awaited us in heaven. This was a big order for a young girl to digest and was hardly consoling; it made me wonder how much more unhappiness I had to face.

Maman Marie and I corresponded regularly. Epinal had been bombed often by the Allies and was partially destroyed. Many of the people I knew had been killed. Food was in short supply, and ration coupons could not always be redeemed. La Mémé periodically gave me provisions, which I sent on to Maman Maire, who was so grateful that she corresponded with the Lassalas family for many years after the war, though they never met.

One could easily have gone hungry with the meager rations during those years. Youngsters up to eighteen were classified as J3, in the period of *croissance* (the growing years). We were entitled to some privileges, such as a chocolate bar once a month. I used to beg God to send my parents back soon, and as a sacrifice I promised him I would give up my chocolate ration. It may seem a small sacrifice in exchange for such a large favor, but I had nothing to offer except my eagerly anticipated piece of chocolate. (Josette never saw an orange or a banana until she came to the United States. As a matter of fact, when we arrived in New York I think we were more amazed by the abundance of food displayed in the stores than by the skyscrapers.) I often wrote to the Red Cross, but that organization carried no clout in Hitler's Germany. The replies to my inquiries about my parents were all the same, polite but "very sorry . . . we do not know . . . be patient." The authorities were trying their best to inquire. If anyone else in France knew the extent of the atrocities being committed in Germany (and I doubt that many did), fortunately I was not aware of them. I still believed my parents were in German work camps. When I felt sorry for myself I used to think of Marceline, who was worse off than I, and then my self-pity would quickly turn into shame.

I had overheard rumors that there were many maquisards hiding in the woods nearby. The Germans must have been warned, because one day they set up camp near Saint-Bonnet and searched the countryside. Most farmers had never yet seen a German soldier. Baptiste looked concerned and was even quieter than usual. He and other men in the village were the liaison for the men hiding in the woods.

A week before the Chaumettes were to leave their summer house, Mrs. Chaumette told me she would like me to come to Clermont-Ferrand to work for her. I politely refused, but I must admit I was flattered. She liked me! Marie, the cook, cried when we parted, but I promised to visit her in Clermont-Ferrand. I did, in fact, visit her several times.

I gladly returned to the farm. The family had acquired two children as boarders for the summer vacation: a young boy of fourteen and his sister, about twelve. Their parents were among the people who came regularly for provisions and had gotten to know the Lassalas family well. They thought it would be good for the children to spend their summer vacation in the country. They were badly in need of some fresh air and wholesome food. The atmosphere in the household was cheerful with all these youngsters. But one night I was suddenly awakened by a commotion in the house. The young girl had gone to bed after what seemed to be a perfectly normal day. She had not complained of anything all day, but started to moan in her sleep. La Mémé looked in on her and noticed blood frothing at the corners of her mouth. The girl died moments later in La Mémé's arms. This tragedy was an emotional blow to each member of the household; for months I could not go to sleep in a dark room. I kept seeing the face of a girl who had survived a war only to fall victim to a virulent illness.

During one of her weekend visits, Bernadette suggested that I come and stay with her and her mother in Clermont-Ferrand. She told me her mother would be delighted to have me. They would help me find a job there, and I could visit Josette on weekends. I had spent most of the money I had made that summer on necessities for Josette and me. Josette didn't relish the idea of my leaving again. She was afraid this time I wouldn't come back. La Mémé, Jeanne, and Baptiste were afraid I would be arrested, but I still had the phony identification card Baptiste had obtained for me. On the strength of that, I convinced them I would be safe. The news from Radio London was good; liberation seemed imminent.

Baptiste, more than anyone else, was upset when I left. By then the Lassalas family thought of me as their own. He couldn't understand why I had to leave. Quite honestly, I thought it would be a healthy change for me. I felt guilty about leaving Josette, but I couldn't help wanting to stay with Bernadette and her mother.

They had a lovely apartment, but life in the city was not as cheerful as I had anticipated. There was no heat, and even though there were three bedrooms in the apartment, we all slept in one bed to keep warm. Food supplies were far from bountiful, but potatoes were filling and we did have a little meat from time to time. We were luckier than most, because we brought food back from Saint-Bonnet each weekend.

Bernadette and her mother weren't wealthy. Bernadette worked in an office for a small salary. As for her mother's antique shop, it cost more to keep than it made, since during wartime people didn't spend their money on antiques. Bernadette's mother wouldn't give up the shop because it had been left to her husband by his parents, and she lived in the hope that when the war was over business would pick up. She opened the store day after day, keeping herself busy cleaning the many beautiful objects and the furniture but only occasionally selling something. Their sole income, then, was Bernadette's salary. Bernadette's brother, a priest, visited his mother and sister rarely because his parish was so far from Clermont-Ferrand. On his visits he would beg his mother to come and live with him, but she would not leave Bernadette.

When I returned to Saint-Bonnet for my first weekend visit, Baptiste told me that Mr. Chaumette had inquired about me. When he heard where I was staying, he asked that I come to his office at City Hall in Clermont-Ferrand. He mentioned to Baptiste that he would be able to get me some free clothing. I was, as I have mentioned, painfully shy and was convinced by then that, as far as the Chaumettes were concerned, I was a little nobody. It would be difficult for me to humble myself before Mr. Chaumette, but I had no clothes suitable for living in a city where, in spite of the shortages, French women still managed to look presentable. I looked plain awful, but at least I was clean. In fact, Jeanne used to tease me about my obsession with hygiene. Since there was no running water in the Lassalas household, bathing was a luxury. The family let me use a barrel in the barn, which I filled with pails of water. This required many trips from the fountain and many pots of water warmed at the fireplace. Then Josette and I, and often little Ririe, would take our weekly bath. I had one Sunday dress and one pair of down-at-the-heel shoes. During the week I wore sabots, wooden clogs not unlike those worn in Holland; a coat borrowed from Jeanne; and one or two dresses not worthy of description.

Because I was so conscious of my appearance I decided to see Mr. Chaumette. I didn't dislike the man; he was the only adult in his family who treated me in a gracious manner, who never corrected me if I didn't address him in the third person. Yet I still felt the sting of humiliation when I entered his office. He politely asked me to sit down and looked at me kindly. His face had never before seemed to look either kind or unkind; he had seemed always to have the same distinguished, polite, but faraway expression. I had never seen this side of him. He told me that he had never fully believed the story that my parents were arrested because of their political views. If the story were true, why had I not remained in Epinal with some friend or relative? To satisfy his curiosity, Mr. Chaumette had made a phone call to the Bureau de Police in Epinal. The truth was out, and I was frankly relieved. I hated telling people lies about my parents' arrest. In my mind, the lies were an admission that any crime was less shameful than the "crime" of being Jewish. Mr. Chaumette assured me that this would be our secret, that he understood and respected my feelings. He also admired Baptiste's discretion in never letting on to him about my true identity. His sincerity was obvious, and I could breathe once again. Mr. Chaumette then gave me some letters authorizing me to go to any store and choose a sensible wardrobe. My newest benefactor insisted that I pay my respects to Mrs. Chaumette as a favor to him. I was so overwhelmed that, although this propect did not particularly appeal to me, I promised to visit his wife the following day. He further insisted that I come to him any time for help with any problem. I was a couragous young lady, he told me, and my parents had raised me well. I don't recall that I said anything but "Thank you, monsieur." He shook my hand and again exacted my promise to visit his wife.

My step was light as I left City Hall. I had never noticed how beautiful Clermont-Ferrand was. I waited for Bernadette at her office so that we could go shopping together. I don't remember anything that I bought except the coat. The coat! It was warm and elegantly cut, although surprisingly modest in price. There it was on a headless mannequin in the window of a small shop. I was afraid the storekeeper would not honor my letter of credit, but Bernadette dragged me in. The saleslady was quite pleasant. Business wasn't too great in those days, and I guess she was glad to see a customer, any customer. Except for the length, the coat was a perfect fit. Before we asked to look at anything else, we showed Mr. Chaumette's letter to the saleswoman, who was impressed. I charged all my purchases to Mr. Chaumette. He trusted me and knew I would not take advantage of his generosity. His trust meant a lot to me. I also had to buy some clothes for Josette.

When I returned to Saint-Bonnet all dressed up for my weekly visit, everyone was flabbergasted. They asked me if I had robbed a store. Before I could explain, La Mémé said in the dialect that I understood quite well by then, "I *knew* we should not have let her go to the big city! I *knew* no good would come of it!" She looked at me and sadly shook her head in disapproval. She knew, of course, that many young peasant girls left their villages to search for a better life in the big city and often ended up living in brothels. La Mémé no doubt figured that was how I had acquired my beautiful new clothes! She nearly fainted with relief when she learned the truth. Josette was thrilled with her new coat and dress, but I felt bad because I had no gifts for little Ririe. I brought her a doll on my next visit. Occasionally, I would take Josette back to the city with me. Bernadette's mother adored her, and Josette loved being fussed over.

I went to visit Mrs. Chaumette at her town house. Only the very, very rich lived in town houses, referred to by the French as *les hôtels particuliers*. The furnishings in the Chaumette town house were even more exquisite than those at the castle. I had asked Bernadette to accompany me for moral support. She, too, was impressed by the tasteful display of wealth. A maid took us to the salon, the formal living room, where Mrs. Chaumette was embroidering. (I had learned from her that aristocrats were never idle; idleness was a luxury in which only the *nouveaux riches* indulged.) Madame was exceedingly gracious to Bernadette and me. She offered us tea. I recall that we were both ill at ease sipping tea with this *grande dame,* but at least she no longer expected me to speak to her in the third person. She asked me if I was working; when I said no, she said that I could work as a governess to the children of her younger daughter, who lived nearby. I thanked her politely and told her I was going to return to Epinal as soon as France was liberated. Bernadette and I were both glad to leave. I had kept my promise to Mr. Chaumette and, besides, his wife wasn't so bad—as long as you didn't work for her.

I never again saw Mr. or Mrs. Chaumette, who had played such an important part in my life. In the Chaumette home I was exposed to hypocrisy, bigotry, and snobbism, but I learned much about etiquette, interior decorating, and even kindness—from the least likely of sources.

Bernadette's mother had heard about a woman from Epinal who was involved in many projects and possibly could give me a job. She had a reputation for being kind and generous. The woman was tall and attractive, although heavily made-up, and was in her early thirties. We went to see her at her home, which mirrored her personality: it was expensive but garish.

The woman's bubbling personality was overwhelming, but I found that I liked her immediately. "If people from Epinal cannot help each other when in need," she said, "the world may as well come to an end!" She gave me a job in one of the stores she owned.

It was a strange business, not unlike an American thrift shop. Clothes were scarce and expensive, and this store provided a place to which the rich could bring their old clothes to sell on consignment. When we sold the clothes, the store received a certain percentage.

The store employed only a manager and me. My benefactor came in rarely and only to collect her profits. She called me "Epinal," a nickname based on our common bond. She always told me she was pleased with my work but that my good performance was what she expected of someone from Epinal. She was always in the company of a much older man who ignored everyone but her and whom she addressed as *"mon chéri."* The manager told me that he was an underworld figure and a collaborator, and that she was his mistress. I was a naive sixteen-year-old by then, and this news upset me. My employer's good heart, however, offset this flaw.

I was not earning a great fortune in my new job, but I was able to pay part of my board and Josette's. La Mémé refused to spend the money I gave her. She put all of it away for me and gave it to me when I left.

I still sorely missed my parents, and I wondered often if the war would ever end. There were times when I thought that the Germans would win and that I would never see Papa or Maman again. In my prayers I still bargained with God. I would deprive myself not only of chocolate, I told him, but also of any small luxuries that came my way so that I would be worthy of God's grace. I got so that every time I had any real fun I felt guilty and gave myself a demerit. Each demerit then required more sacrifice to redeem myself. Uncle Leon had surely left his mark when he scolded me for enjoying myself while my parents were prisoners.

Mr. Fritz, a German Jew, and his Gentile wife lived in hiding in Saint-Bonnet in a small apartment over a barn near the farmhouse. Mrs. Fritz sewed and baked for the village women, who, in return, provided all the Fritzes' food. Mr. Fritz was a chemist whose talent at making soap—a rare commodity in wartime France—from beef suet and lye made him somewhat of a local legend. Neither of us admitted to the other that we were Jewish, but we both knew, and there was a great rapport between us.

Mr. Fritz had a great sense of humor, and everyone liked him. He was a gifted musician whose Sunday afternoon accordion recitals in empty barns delighted the young people who came from the surrounding villages to dance to his music. He had played for us when we staged our celebrated variety show.

La Mémé ruled the household with an iron fist, and Baptiste was positively fatherly when it came to my social activities. People referred to me as *une belle gamine* (a good-looking kid), and my being a city girl was an added attraction to the many young men in our village, who whistled at me more than once. I was not allowed to attend the Sunday dances unchaperoned, of course. Every girl in the village was chaperoned, often by both parents.

La bourée is a folk dance of Auvergne that is performed primarily by men. When coaxed, Baptiste and some of his contemporaries would oblige us with a performance. The dance was a sight to behold. I enjoyed dancing more than anything else, but Uncle Leon's words kept ringing in my ears, and of course I felt guilty every time my toes tickled a dance floor. Guilty or not, I went dancing every chance I had.

Mr. Maurice, who had been a regular visitor, stopped coming to the farmhouse when he and his family moved from Vichy to Clermont-Ferrand. I went to his home to inquire about him and learned that he and his family had been picked up by the gestapo.

He and his family never came back, and as I write this my heart is filled with sadness and gratitude. That Josette and I are alive we owe in large part to his goodness.

Little by little, we noticed fewer Germans in Clermont-Ferrand. We had heard in the transmission from

Radio London that Rommel had his problems in Africa and that the Germans were losing ground on the Russian front and in the Italian theater. We deduced that they needed reinforcement on both fronts. The French newspapers were censored, of course, and their reports on the war were always slanted in favor of the Germans. (By then, of course, the United States had long been fighting on the side of the Allies.) Even the Radio London reports were understated to keep useful information from the Germans, so we were kept pretty much in the dark.

Apparently the German leaders were pulling soldiers from our area and sending them to the front. Soon in Clermont-Ferrand the only reminder of occupation was the big German flag hanging over the door of the *Kommandantur.*

Early one morning Bernadette, her mother, and I were awakened by loud shouts from the street. We all ran to the windows and opened the shutters. It was barely daylight. People were dancing and screaming with joy. Many were still in their night clothes. Every window opened and bewildered people looked out, to hear *"Les Allies ont debarques en Normandie!"* It was D day, June 6, 1944. English, American, and Free French troops had landed on French soil in Normandy.

No matter how tragic or happy one's life has been, there are moments that stand out, to be remembered for a lifetime as the happiest and most glorious. I have many—most notably when my son Paul, my daughter Michele, and my granddaughter Lauren Beth were born. But D day is in a class by itself, a memory that I and most of my contemporaries would classify as sublime.

We dressed quickly and ran out into the streets to join the old, the young, the children, who were all singing "La Marseillaise," the national anthem. We decided to go to

Saint-Bonnet that night to celebrate there. The maquisards came out of hiding, and it was then that Jeanne first told me about Baptiste's activities in the movement. I was so happy, all I could think about was that my parents would soon be released from the camp to come back to join us.

Of course the Germans did not gracefully retreat, and France was not liberated overnight. Many lives were lost along the rest of the arduous road. Military cemeteries all over France remind us that the taste of victory is bittersweet. Paris wasn't liberated until August 25, 1944, almost three months later. Technically, in Clermont-Ferrand, as in many other parts of France, we were still in occupied territory, and the few Germans crossing our region on their way to the front were angrier than ever. Taking prisoners was a thing of the past; now they simply shot people without ceremony.

The Allies landed in southern France near the port of Toulon on August 15, 1944, thereby sandwiching in the German troops from the northwest and the southeast. French soil became a battleground. Cities were destroyed, bombed by the Allies, and many more lives were lost.

I grew weary of it all, and like everyone else I was impatient for the war's end. It would take a little longer than I had anticipated for my parents to be freed. I was filled with mixed emotions: the anticipation of joy at being reunited with Papa and Maman and the fear that my parents would be disappointed in me. Papa in his last letter has asked me to guard their wordly goods, and I was by this time penniless. I hoped they wouldn't be too angry. At least I had saved Josette: they had to be proud of me for that.

It was not until March 21, 1945, that the Allies and Free French troops stepped on German soil. Nine months had elapsed since D day. It had been a long winter. It was even more difficult to obtain food. France was in turmoil. Many of its cities were destroyed; trains were used mostly by the armies, and civilian transportation was at a standstill. Bare necessities became luxuries. Most homes were unheated. By then we ate mostly potatoes and cheese and some eggs we brought back from Saint-Bonnet, but we were so cold that we kept our coats on indoors at all times. Yet we considered ourselves privileged to have some decent food. La Mémé knitted me some heavy wool underwear, which I kept for many years as a memento.

Maman Marie's letters were not encouraging. The Collinses were still in occupied territory in eastern France, and had not yet seen the Allies. Epinal, which was bombed constantly, was a shambles. Eventually the Allies reached the East, but in her letters Maman Marie begged me to be patient and not to return yet. She said that sometimes the Allies were there; then fighting would resume, and the next day the Germans would be back for a while.

I was impatient as only a sixteen-year-old can be. I had thought D day would mark the end of the war and that France would be liberated instantly. The Third Reich did not surrender until May 7, 1945, eleven months after D day. Victory was won—at an astronomical price. War had been declared in Europe on September 3, 1939. Six years of hell. For many, like Josette and me, the war completely changed the course of our lives. After a long and difficult period of readjustment, many, fortunately, were able to pick up the pieces and resume a normal life. For some, however, the scars were too deep.

The day World War II ended was a day of indescribable joy. The physical suffering war causes was technically over—but another kind of suffering was about to begin. It would last for many years in the European countries that had been ravaged by Hitler and his armies. Food supplies didn't become plentiful overnight; it took many years to rebuild the cities.

As the Allies advanced into Germany, the prisoners of war, the young men in labor camps, and those Jews and others who had survived the concentration camps were repatriated to their own countries. In store for those who were fortunate enough to be reunited with family was delirious joy. But many had been separated for as long as five years. Children had become men and women, strangers to their fathers and mothers; women who where once docile housewives had become both mothers and fathers in their husbands' absence. These women had taken complete charge of their households; they could not return to their former roles the moment their spouses returned. This caused tremendous conflict in tradition-bound relationships. The released prisoners and those who had escaped imprisonment had aged, had suffered; all were different people, and many had grown apart. The anticipation of being reunited had sustained them through the long years of the war, but the reality of reunion resulted in psychological turbulence that some overcame but many did not.

The Allies and the Germans were still fighting on French soil. My impatience grew. Papa and Maman would look for me at Maman Marie's, and I wanted to be there with Josette when they arrived. Against the advice of everyone who feared for our safety, I decided to return with Josette to Epinal. This was the end of my relationship with Bernadette as it had been. We all somehow knew that, even if I came back, things could never be the same, and so our parting was awkward. Bernadette and her mother walked us through a sprinkling of January snow to the station. When I bought our tickets I was told that it would be difficult to reach Epinal. There was no train schedule, everything was in an uproar, and the ticket agent tried to discourage me. But I had made up my mind and could not be dissuaded. I simply *had* to be home when our parents arrived. The good-byes at the station were filled with great emotion and tears. Josette and I waved to the two wonderful women standing on the platform. They waved back until we could no longer see them, and then I cried for a long time. Josette cried, too, but only because she saw me cry. She was, of course, too young to understand, at only six-and-a-half.

We boarded a Paris-bound train. It was filled to capacity and, as usual, we attracted the attention of some of our fellow passengers. I particularly remember a Jewish couple who had been in hiding and were returning to their home in Paris after several years. They were concerned for our safety and thought I was crazy to undertake such a dangerous journey, especially with little Josette. I had but one thought in mind: to reach Epinal. In spite of the many obstacles in our path I knew we would succeed. La Mémé had given us food for the trip: cheese, salami, and a large loaf of bread. This had to last us until we reached Epinal, so we ate sparingly. I was almost ashamed to be so fortunate. The other passengers eyed our food: some stared openly, their mouths actually drooling. They were eating, too, but nothing as extravagant as salami and cheese. I felt positively gluttonous.

Our train made several stops and soon became so crowded that people were forced to sit on their suitcases in the aisles. We had been riding for several hours when the train came to a sudden stop. We were smack in the middle of the countryside, and then we heard the train conductor shouting, "Everyone get off!" The retreating Germans had blown up the suspension bridge over the wide river, and the only remaining crossing was a smaller bridge some miles away. Only a limited number of buses were available, and elderly people and women with small children had priority. No one was permitted to take luggage. I had two choices: to abandon my suitcase and go on the bus with Josette or to walk. It was too long a stretch for Josette, so the woman I had befriended offered to take Josette on the bus with her, and her husband and I would walk with our luggage. Of course Josette screamed and cried, as she always did when we were separated. When I insisted, she went reluctantly.

It was a long walk through the fields, and my suitcase became heavier with each step. The others could not help me, burdened as they were with their own bags. The pain in my shoulder from carrying the heavy bag in the bitter cold soon spread throughout my body. When we finally reached the other side of the smaller bridge, I was dragging my suitcase, and my gloveless hands were frostbitten. Josette was still crying when I found her. The woman had been unable to calm her. There was no train waiting for us on the other side, and passengers from a previous train were waiting as well. There were no houses or villages in sight. We were stranded in the middle of nowhere. The bus driver told us to be patient, that a train would come sooner or later, but normal service had not yet been reestablished. We were so cold that we ran around to keep warm and talked to each other to keep busy. When our train finally arrived many hours later, we would have welcomed a cattle train. Josette neither complained nor gave me any trouble.

We arrived at the Gare de Lyon in Paris in the dark of early morning. To reach Epinal we had to catch a train at the Gare de l'Est, at the other end of Paris. I don't remember how we got there, perhaps by bus or the *métro*. At any rate, when we reached the station it was practically deserted, and when I went to purchase our tickets for Epinal the man looked at me incredulously. Had I lost my mind? his expressions seemed to ask. The normal procedure was to board a train to Nancy, a two-and-a-half-hour ride from Paris, and change, usually on the same platform, for a train bound to Epinal, another half-hour or so away. But that was the route when things were normal. To the ticket seller's knowledge, the trains leaving Paris went no farther than Reims, but he thought perhaps with luck I could find some mode of transportation from there. He asked me if I knew anyone in Paris who could take us in until the train schedules resumed a semblance of normalcy. When I told him I knew no one in Paris, he shrugged and said, "I don't know what to tell you. Besides, you are crazy to attempt to go east. There's still fighting going on there." He called the station master, who asked us to come to his office. I had to tell him my whole story to make him understand why it was so important for me to reach Epinal. Somehow, I wasn't afraid; in spite of the negative answers, I knew we were going to reach Epinal safely. I am not stubborn, yet even now, when faced with a problem, I will not give up until I find a solution. The station master suggested that we board a train to Reims and play it by ear from there.

Our train wasn't to leave for several hours. Josette and I went to the station restaurant for a hot drink. By then we were colder and more tired than ever. Fortified with the hot liquid, Josette slept until it was time to board the train. I knew we had arrived in Reims when I saw from afar the spire of the famed cathedral towering over the city. The only train leaving the station was a local going to Troyes, farther east. If we took that, we would at least be going in the right direction. I had been to Troyes with Papa many times. It was an industrial city with many spinning mills where Papa purchased goods for his business each season. I knew we were getting closer to Epinal. I don't recall how many trains we took before we reached Neufchâteau, where our transportation came to a temporary standstill. The kindly *chef de gare* there suggested that we wait at the Café de la Gare across the way. He said he would let us know when a train was to leave in the direction of Epinal. He thought that would not happen for several hours.

That café stands out in my memory because it was there that our first American GI spoke to us. I had seen several American soldiers in the train station in Paris, and my heart was filled with warmth when I first laid eyes on our liberators. The American *laissez-aller* (relaxed attitude) contrasted sharply with the severe, stiff, superior behavior of the Germans. I asked the barmaid if we could wait until we were able to board a train. As usual we attracted her attention and curiosity. By then our food and money were almost gone. The lady felt sorry for *les pauvres petites gosses.* We must have been some sight to behold: tired, hungry, and train-grimy kids. The perfect picture of two orphans.

The woman brought us some food, which we ate hungrily, but my attention was riveted on tables occupied by our noisy and cheerful liberators. The English language was completely foreign to me then, but I sat watching them and listening, and I probably forgot about my train for a while. One lone soldier, a large black man, kept smiling at us. I will never forget his kind, beautiful face. He finally walked over to us and offered us our first Hershey bar, which we gratefully accepted. The candy was followed by chewing gum and other goodies from his army bag. I was not at all reluctant to converse with our generous GI. Quite on the contrary, it was my first conversation with one of our benefactors. Our hearts were filled with love and admiration for the Americans in those days. They had liberated us from Nazi oppression, which was not something the French took for granted. GIs all over France were welcomed with open arms as guests in most homes. In return for our hospitality they showered us with products from the PX, and we gratefully accepted these luxuries. I think the French were the only ones who could make K rations into a gourmet meal.

I do not know how the GI and I were able to communicate, as neither one of us spoke the other's language, but we managed. He kept looking at Josette, and the only French word I remember him saying was, *"jolie, jolie."*

Josette and I finally boarded a train, and in time we reached Golbey, a small town near Epinal, no more than five kilometers from the city line. Somehow, we got a ride in a truck, and the kind driver took us to Chantraine. He left us at the bottom of the hill called Route de Bains. I left our suitcase at a nearby grocery, and we walked to the Collins home. It had taken us two and a half days of sleeping on trains and in train stations, and finally hitchhiking, but we had made it home and were looking forward to a brighter future.

Two and a half years had elapsed since we left our hometown. The Collinses didn't know I was coming. When

Guiguite opened the door, she was stunned. When she regained her composure she started to scream with joy and grabbed both Josette and me, which brought the rest of the family. Maman Marie kept saying, "My beautiful Josette has finally come home." It was an emotional moment for all of us, with lots of tears. We had so much to talk about. The house was just as I remembered it. Maman Marie looked a little older and a little thinner.

Maman Marie had two new boarders, an illegitimate baby boy about six months old, and Cri-Cri, a beautiful little girl of five who had been in an orphanage until recently and had become hard to handle. The nuns had begged Maman Marie to take her; patience, firmness, and much love had transformed her into an adorable child by the time we arrived.

Papa Auguste, who was still at work when we arrived, came home some time later. He was so overcome with joy that he couldn't speak. He cradled Josette in his arms for a long time. That evening, the Thiriets visited, and there were more tears. We were home.

I wished the Lassalas family, Bernadette, and her mother were here, too. Raymond Thiriet was a lieutenant in the Free French army and would be home soon on a short furlough. We stayed up late that night, catching up on the past two and half years. Then they scolded me for being so impatient: fighting was still going on in and near Epinal, and we could have been killed.

Papa Auguste and Maman Marie's modest two-bedroom house was lovely and located in a beautiful area, but it was somewhat crowded with all of us. The Thiriets invited me to stay with them across the street. I didn't mind at all. I loved their daughter Jacqueline and was secretly in love with their son Raymond. The Thiriets were kind and loving people and were fond of me. Josette stayed at the Collinses and, for the first time in a long time, did not mind being separated from me. She, too, knew she was home.

I shared a room with Jacqueline, who was about three years older than I. She loved playing big sister to me, and I felt comfortable. Jacqueline and I were in and out of the Collins home, and Josette and I never missed a day without spending some time together. She and Cri-Cri adjusted well to each other. All was well on the eastern front. I wrote to the Lassalas family and Bernadette immediately to let them know we had arrived safely.

The Allies continued to push the Germans farther from our region, and the area became safer. Still, fighting continued in France. In the Ardennes, a raging battle lasted for a long time until the Allies finally pushed the Germans back across the border. We listened daily for news of the Allies' progress, realizing that the farther they went into Germany the sooner prisoners would be liberated. Would my parents be among the first to return?

A few days after we returned, I went with Guiguite and Jacqueline to Epinal. As we reached the city I gasped in disbelief. Most of the center of town had been demolished, either during air raids or during the battles that took place in its streets. Mutilated buildings stood like monstrous skeletons, and rubble lay everywhere. Some streets were entirely closed off to cars and pedestrians in case some of the standing ruins began to crumble. Epinal was five hundred years old; fortunately, the Basilique Saint-Maurice, which dated back to the Middle Ages, was spared, but Notre Dame, an equally beautiful church, was completely destroyed. We walked over to the Rue des Minimes, where my family had lived. One side of the street had been destroyed. The facade of our building was still intact, but the inside of the house was partially destroyed by bombing and was uninhabitable. Some of the rooms we had lived in had no floor, but my parents' bedroom and the family dining room were spared. I stood there and finally realized I would never again live there. I almost wished no part of the building was left to remind me of happier times. On my way out, I noticed the mailbox and its brass plate that bore our name. I thought how sad my parents would be not to have a home to return to. We stopped at Maman Marie's on the way back. I cried uncontrollably when I told her about our home. I knew then it *would* have been better if the building had been completely destroyed; as it was, I had to look at the shell of what had once been the home of a happy family.

Maman Marie took me into her dining room to talk to me privately. She said she had wanted to speak to me alone for a long time but had not found the courage. She then warned me that my parents might have died in camp and that I should consider that possibility in planning our future. I thought she had gone crazy. Hoping to console me with something she truly believed from her Christian Science philosophy, she continued, "If your parents are dead, they are among the lucky ones. They have earned their place in heaven for eternity. Someday we will join them, when we have paid our own dues here on earth, our hell and testing grounds." I loved and respected Maman Marie; she had often discussed her religious beliefs with me. Clearly the members of her family, including Papa Auguste, humored her, never contradicted her, and let her talk until she realized that they were just listening to be polite. Then she would comment, "It takes longer for some to be convinced," and would go about her business.

But this time Maman Marie had gone too far, and I ran out of the house and over to the Thiriets' home in tears. Between sobs, I related our conversation to Mrs. Thiriet. I can still see her face before me: her eyes were solemn and betrayed what she was actually thinking, but her voice chirped, "Oh, you know Mrs. Collins! She often exaggerates, and as for her beliefs, no one pays any attention to them." Maman Marie tried to prepare me and went about it in the best way she knew how. Mrs. Thiriet, faced with my sorrow, tried to encourage me in spite of her private opinions. I couldn't accept the possibility that my parents wouldn't come back. So, I chose to believe Mrs. Thiriet. Deep down, however, I knew when I looked into her eyes that she was thinking along the same lines as Maman Marie.

Maman Marie was an extrovert. What she thought was immediately on her tongue. Perhaps she was not always diplomatic, but her words were never meant to hurt. Mrs. Thiriet, on the other hand, was more reserved. A devout Catholic, she never argued with her friend about religion and would patiently listen to Maman Marie's tirades at least once a day.

They were the closest of friends. One complemented the other. In the French custom, they always called each other "madame." Good manners, respect, and deference were simply signs of being civilized.

I had attended Mass every Sunday with the Lassalas and had grown to enjoy it. When I moved in with the Thiriets, I felt a little lonely at home on Sundays when Mrs. Thiriet and Jacqueline left for church, so I decided to join them. Mrs. Thiriet was absolutely delighted, but my going to Mass greatly displeased Maman Marie, who vehemently voiced her feelings. Perhaps because she had been unsuccessful in interesting me in her religion, one of her statements was meant to hit me hard: "There is no longer a need for you to pass as a Catholic, and at this point your parents would be displeased if they knew you attended Catholic services." I was caught between the proverbial rock and hard place: I found solace and enjoyment at Mass, but I now felt guilty about going, fearing that my parents would be angry. When I returned to church the following Sunday, I suddenly felt I did not belong. I did not go after that, and Mrs. Thiriet never asked my reasons.

Raymond, now twenty-three, came home some time thereafter, looking more handsome than ever in his uniform. I had always had a crush on him, but only Guiguite and Jacqueline were aware of it. Raymond was six years older than I and probably had never looked at me before. Much to his surprise, I had grown into a young lady and was, according to the consensus, *une belle fille*. I did not share this opinion. I had by then a full-fledged inferiority complex, and I felt like an ugly duckling. I was torn apart by the loss of my parents and by being different from other girls. I tried never to displease anyone in whose home I was a guest, so grateful was I that they had taken in both Josette and me. But it is difficult to please everyone *and* God, who sees all. One becomes too scrupulous: I even felt guilty when I had unkind *thoughts* about anyone!

I lived for the day when my parents would return and we could resume a normal life, but I wondered if my parents would be pleased with my performance during the past three years. I couldn't confide in anyone. I was simply too unsure of myself. Mrs. Thiriet probably would have been the most understanding; she truly loved me and was, in my opinion, the closest a human being could get to being a saint on earth.

Raymond was his parents' pride and joy. He had a much older half brother (from Mr. Thiriet's previous marriage), who was married and lived far from Epinal. The brother was not a frequent visitor to their home, having made his career in the army and having lived in the French colonies for many years. Raymond had earned his officer's stripes and many decorations, but, like many soldiers, he was modest and rarely talked about his wartime exploits.

Encouraged by both his parents, he took me to the movies while he was on furlough. I was so shy that I blushed more than I care to remember, but Raymond was kind and understanding, and in the months to come I began to feel at ease in his presence. By the time he told me he loved me, I had long considered myself his. The Thiriets and the Collinses were so pleased when we told them. But Raymond was stationed in Germany and seldom came home, so our romance developed mostly on paper, through our daily correspondence. Nevertheless, our romance made my life normal, made me feel the way a young girl, in different times and circumstances, should feel.

Mr. Thiriet, who worked as the head of a government office in Epinal, got me a job in one of his offices. I was the only girl among five or six long-married men and one older bachelor. I was treated with such kindness and deference by the gentlemen in the office—even by the chief, whom everyone else hated—that my timidity soon dissolved. The function of our office was to distribute ration stamps and do the bookkeeping involved therein. I know adding machines existed in those days, but we didn't have any, and I spent hours adding the longest columns I had ever seen. To this day, although multiplying is not my forte, I can add faster than anyone I know!

Josette returned to school in Chantraine and was happy. I visited her several times a day, at lunchtime, on

[127]

my way back to work and often at dinner with the Collinses. Guiguite, Jacqueline, and I were an inseparable threesome. I corresponded regularly with the Lassalas and Bernadette, and I dreamed of the day my parents and I would visit them.

Raymond had corresponded with Tante Regine in the United States during the war to give her news of her family. He continued to write after the war. One day a letter from her awaited me when I returned from work. I was overjoyed to hear from her. She was going to send us packages, and she had enclosed a check in the letter. She mentioned that she wasn't rich, but she was going to try her best to send me money. I immediately replied that the packages would be welcome but that I was working and didn't need any money. Actually, I earned very little, but the Thiriets and the Collinses refused to charge me for my board or Josette's, and, except for clothing, my needs were minimal. I was certainly not spoiled and required very little.

Epinal was an animated city once again. Its streets were filled with GIs. Our gratitude toward the Americans was unbounded. Most households invited some of them to share their meals and spend quiet family evenings. The GIs were happy to accept such invitations. They were glad to be part of a family, since they missed their own. The Collins and Thiriet homes were always filled with soldiers. Maman Marie started to do the GIs' laundry, and they repaid her with provisions of all kinds. Meals were no longer skimpy at 37 Route de Bains. As a matter of fact, Maman Marie shared provisions with her less fortunate neighbors. Some GIs came to visit me, since Tante Regine had given my address to everyone she knew (or knew of) who was stationed in Europe. Some left for the front, never to be seen again; others came back on

[128]

their furloughs. I particularly remember one American who spoke German; he and I were able to communicate quite well. He seemed skeptical when I told him about my experiences after the Germans arrested my parents. But after he had been to Germany and witnessed the horrors of the camps, he came back to Epinal especially to apologize to me. He admitted that he at first thought I had invented the story I told him, and he was ashamed of himself for doubting me.

By then, I was well aware of what had taken place in the concentration camps. The whole world was numb from the horror of it all. The news couldn't be hidden from me; it was, after all, the main topic in newspapers and on the radio. My world was crumbling, and once again I started to make deals with God. I would settle for one parent, I told him, but if it had to be just one, please let it be Papa. I missed Maman, of course, but I had a stronger yearning for Papa.

All the prisoners of war were being returned to their respective countries, not an easy task for the Allied forces. Against everyone's judgment, I decided that I would go to Paris to await the returning convoys. One of Maman Marie's neighbors had a sister who lived in Paris. She agreed to take Josette and me into her home so that we could go to the station daily to await the convoys' arrivals. Josette and I went to the Gare de l'Est and waited on the crowded platform for the first train to arrive. Many other anxious people were standing there, hoping their loved ones would return. The Red Cross, the police, movie crews, photographers, and reporters were everywhere. Everyone looked in the direction from which the train was to arrive. Finally, the train chugged into the station, which was soon filled with the utter silence that only shock produces. The first prisoners stepped onto the platform. They looked like walking skeletons. Their heads were shaved; their eyes were sunken and dull. Most still wore their striped suits. Others wore U.S. Army uniforms. Many had to be carried on stretchers; some supported one another. In spite of the medical care and food they had received after the army liberated the camps, most were still so weak they could hardly walk. If D day stands out as the most memorable day in my life, this day remains the most painful, filled as it was with such incredible horror. Thirty-six years have passed since I stood there holding Josette's hand, and I still find it difficult to describe what I saw. People began to scream and cry, and the police had to restrain the crowds. Some recognized a member of their family, but the majority did not. Our parents, of course, were not on this first convoy, or on the next, or on any other. A member of the committee who received the prisoners advised me to go home. He took my name and address and promised to get in touch with me in the event that he located my parents. I kept thinking that perhaps they were among the sick carried out on stretchers, or that I just didn't recognize them when they passed by. How could anyone recognize a walking skeleton? My hopes weren't completely shattered. Some prisoners were still hospitalized in Germany, too sick to be moved. Some were displaced.

The ride back to Epinal was grim. I had anticipated a triumphal return. Now my imagination started to run wild. My parents had lost their memories, or perhaps they had escaped to Russia. I thought of any possibility in order to avoid a painful reality.

I bombarded the Red Cross with letters in the hope that they could locate my parents. They answered that they could only give me the names and addresses of five people who had returned and had been in camp with my parents. I wrote to these people, and most answered me. They were extremely sorry that my parents had not come back as yet, and they wished me well. Except for two men, they had never met my parents. One had spent some time with Papa but lost track of him when they were sent to different labor camps. The other, Mr. Henri, did not write but came instead to see me in Epinal. He and Papa had become true friends in camp and he had promised to look me up in the event he returned first. Papa and Mr. Henri had worked in a salt mine together.

Prisoners at this mine, as long as they were able to stand up and were capable of performing their duties, were not exterminated. According to Mr. Henri, a gestapo committee visited the camp weekly. Prisoners had to stand in the courtyard like soldiers on parade. Loudspeakers announced that those who were ill and wished medical care should step out of the line and board trucks that would take them to the hospital where they would be well cared for. At first, many went, believing the announcement, but those who remained soon realized that no one who went for "medical care" ever came back. They correctly assumed that those who left were exterminated. Very few stepped out of the line thereafter, unless they were desperate or barely able to stand up. Prisoners worked under the worst conditions: long hours and barely enough food to survive. According to Mr. Henri, Papa contracted typhus, one of the major illnesses in the camp. He fought it and kept working, but he became so ill that one week before the camp was liberated he stepped out of the line. One week.

As for Maman, no one was able to find any trace of her whatsoever. I learned only that both she and Papa were deported from France to Auschwitz. She was recuperating from surgery when she was arrested, and she was obviously not strong enough to work.

I accumulated all this information, but I did not accept the fact that my parents had died, and for many years I continued to have fantasies that they had escaped to Russia, lost their memories, and were unable to communicate with us, but that eventually they would return.

If someone you love dies from an illness or as a result of an accident, the shock and grief are most painful for the survivor, but viewing the body (or at least a casket) and partaking in all the traditional rituals before the burial help the survivor to accept the fact that death is final. After a period of mourning, no matter how painful and long, one attempts to resume living. But, as I saw it, my parents didn't really die; they just did not come back. I couldn't accept that they had died: there was no funeral, no bodies to view, no grave to visit. How could I even mourn them properly?

By then people referred to Josette and me as *les orphelines*. I wondered why God had let me down. Wasn't I worthy of his grace? My opinion of myself diminished even more. I couldn't accept being pitied as an orphan. In spite of the kind people surrounding us and the prospect of marrying Raymond, I was miserable. I had never thought the war would end this way.

My life for the last four years had been bearable only because I had lived for the day my parents, Josette, and I would be reunited and resume living as we had in the past. Jewish families who had been spared started to return to Epinal, and Josette and I soon became the objects of their pity. Soon, meeting anyone who had known my parents became unbearable to me. They invariably

showered me with advice on what to do and what not to
do.

When it became common knowledge that I was engaged to Raymond, it was even more difficult for me to
face anyone. The criticism that I encountered was con-
fusing and painful. I was practically accused of committing some sort of religious treason because Raymond was
not Jewish. How could I even think of marrying a Catholic when Christians had killed my parents merely because
they were Jewish? Did those people not owe their lives, as
I did, to Christians who sheltered them all through the
war?

Worse than their criticism of my engagement were
their words: "Your parents have been killed." How could
they be so sure? Were they there to witness their last
hours? The same know-it-alls went on to say, "If your parents were alive, they would object strongly to your marrying outside your faith." What faith? My parents had
raised me to believe in God, to obey the Ten Commandments, to be kind and charitable to others in order to live
with dignity. My parents' friends were from all faiths.
Why would they be angry now? But the seeds of doubt
and guilt were planted; the last thing I wanted was to displease my parents, dead or alive. I was convinced that if
there was a remote possibility that they had been killed,
they were looking at Josette and me from heaven.

I was thoroughly confused. I had not been raised in a
traditional Jewish environment. My parents were proud
of their Jewish heritage even though we did not observe
every Sabbath by praying in a synagogue. We celebrated
religious holidays at home for tradition's sake, and often
our non-Jewish friends observed with us. They, in return,
invited us to their holiday festivities. Therefore, I was

[133]

equally at ease with Jews and non-Jews and was, after the war, more familiar with Catholic rituals than with those of my own faith.

I was impressionable and idealistic at seventeen and was of course upset that the religious issue had been raised. I didn't need to carry more guilt. I wondered constantly if my parents would approve of my conduct during the last three years, especially of the way I had managed the little money I recovered; this was an added burden. When I was with the Collinses and the Thiriets, my true, kind friends, I was part of two loving families. The people who criticized and advised me considered themselves truly superior, in many respects, to the Collinses and "the likes of them" and therefore dismissed them as easily as they would a delivery man. The Collinses had served their purpose, my "friends" implied; they had taken Josette and me in as part of their family, but when it came to advising us, they just did not have the necessary intelligence or interest.

Fortunately, I was able to recognize my true friends, and I avoided the do-gooders as much as I could in a town as small as Epinal. One exception was a family called the Engelsiques, who were most kind and understanding at all times, and who comforted me on many occasions. They eventually adopted a young girl who had lost her parents in a concentration camp, even though they had children of their own.

Raymond and I planned to be married in a year, but when I wrote to Tante Regine to announce the happy event, her answer was disturbing. She felt I was too young to make such an important decision. She begged me to come to America with Josette and suggested that if I still loved Raymond after a reasonable period, we could consider two options: I could return to France, or Raymond could come to America, where she would give us the most beautiful wedding. She then wrote to Raymond and asked him, for his sake and my own, to encourage me to take her advice.

To his parents' and my surprise, Raymond was in favor of following Tante Regine's suggestion. He spoke perfect English and was impressed with the United States. He had made many American friends in the army and was convinced that with his educational background he could apply for and receive a good position in the American embassy in Washington. To him, the possibility of a life in foreign service was attractive.

At first I was disappointed, but Raymond was insistent. He was stationed in the occupied French sector in Germany and wouldn't be discharged for some time. He felt that we certainly would have a much better future in the land of plenty, and so should wait.

Tante Regine used every weapon at her disposal to convince me to come to America. She was the spokesperson for Papa's family, none of whom could write English, and they too wanted us to leave France. At first I wasn't at all thrilled with the idea of leaving. The war was over, and Josette and I were among friends; our lives were no longer in danger. I had a job, and I was going to be married. What if my parents came back and found us not at home but in the United States, so far away?

Tante Regine's letters kept coming, with promises of *la dolce vita* in the United States. According to her, some members of Papa's family were very wealthy. Josette and I would be, to quote her exactly, "dressed in silk and velvet." She said that she had moved from a one-bedroom apartment to larger quarters just so that she would have room for us when we arrived. I remembered the days when Regine lived with us and how much I loved her—almost as much as I loved Maman. She had virtually raised me, and I was suddenly filled with an uncontrollable desire to see her and be with her again. If strangers had been so kind to me, it would be heaven to be among loving relatives, who could only be kinder. I remembered, too, that in his last letter Papa had told me to go to America. He must have felt that we would be well cared for by our family.

My decision to leave France was most influenced by my longing to be with Tante Regine. Her letters were filled with love and promises of a utopian life, and it was hard at seventeen not to be impressed. I became disenchanted with my life in Epinal, where I was constantly reminded of my parents. I could always come back to France if I didn't like the States.

But what finally prompted me to leave France was the realization that I was more in love with love than with Raymond, my absentee fiancé, who came home on rare furloughs and with whom I conducted a courtship by mail. At first the prospect of marriage seemed to offer solutions to all my problems, since I couldn't resume a normal life with my parents. When the option to leave for America became more and more attractive to me, I realized that perhaps it would be best if I waited to make a decision about Raymond until I was settled in the States.

Right before I decided to leave, an American soldier came to visit me at the Thiriets' home, at Tante Regine's request, and tried to convince me further. He certainly was quite insistent: "Your parents died because they were Jewish. How could you entertain the idea of marrying a non-Jewish man?" I was angered by what I considered his presumptuous behavior, but I kept my thoughts to myself. All these people could think about was that Raymond wasn't Jewish. Didn't they realize that, without people like the Collinses, the Lassalas, and Bernadette's family, Josette and I and many more Jews would not be alive? These people had put their lives on the line for us, and every Jew who had been in hiding and survived the war had at least one Christian family to thank. I hated that kind of thinking. It simply perpetuated hatred among men.

About the time I had made my decision, Mrs. Rosemberg telephoned me: Marceline was alive! Josette and I went immediately to Gourdon.

My cousin Jacqueline met us at the train station. Mr. Rosemberg had been killed in a concentration camp, she told us. Marie and Susan had survived, and Henri was still in the army. Marceline had regained some of her physical strength but rarely spoke to anyone.

From outside, Gourdon looked as beautiful and peaceful as it had two years before. Nothing was changed; the house and the grounds looked the same. Before I entered the house, however, I knew that inside nothing was the same. Mr. Rosemberg was gone and, because of his absence, no one—and nothing—would ever be the same again. The Germans had occupied the castle and had done extensive damage to the inside. They had stolen most of the antiques and left some rooms completely bare.

My cousin received us warmly and was genuinely happy to see us again. As usual, the house was filled with guests, perhaps more guests now to help the family forget that one of its cherished members would never return. Mrs. Rosemberg was concerned mostly with Marceline, who had become withdrawn and remained in her room most of the time. The main reason she summoned me to the castle was in the hope that I might be able to help Marceline come out of her shell.

I found Marceline lying on the floor in her room, staring at the ceiling. She had slept on a board for so long that she couldn't get used to sleeping on a soft mattress. Although her face showed some happiness when she caught sight of me, she did not get up to embrace me. I remember vividly what she said: "I wanted you to be here because I know you will be the only one to understand." Her hair was quite short; it had been shaved and was growing back in little curls all over her head. Her beautiful brown eyes were sunken, and she looked thin and frail. Without any coaxing from me, she told me all her experiences from her arrest until she was released and reunited with her family. She grieved for her father, who had been interned in the same camp. When she finished, I was overwhelmed by a deep sense of shame. How could I ever have felt sorry for myself? Nothing I had experienced during the war came close to what she had had to endure. She did not seem to feel self-pity. Marceline was always the intellectual, and I was the *débrouillarde,* the one with "street smarts." As far back as I could remember, she always read avidly and had a keen interest in the world around her. I learned a lot from her and can remember many nights we sat talking until dawn.

Her family was, of course, overjoyed that she had been returned safely to them. They were trying perhaps too hard, however, to make her feel at home again.

Marceline said that she would have preferred to stay in a rehabilitation center with other former prisoners until she could face the "normal" life outside. The transition from horror to normalcy had been too rapid, and her family was smothering her with concern. She hoped I would be able to make them understand that she needed time to adjust, to accept being among them again. Her mother's main concern was that Marceline refused to sleep in her bed and spent most of her time lying on the floor. She couldn't understand that sleeping arrangements were the least of the adjustments Marceline had to make. Her family couldn't understand her need for a period of readjustment and so showered her with too much kindness, which simply angered Marceline and increased her frustration.

I convinced Mrs. Rosemberg to respect Marceline's wishes, to let her come around on her own terms. She finally understood what motivated her daughter's behavior, and, although concerned, she was rather relieved and promised to be patient. She realized that the past could not be swept under the rug and forgotten. The time Marceline had spent in a concentration camp was branded in her memory for as long as she lived, just like the number that was tattooed on her arm. Marceline and I spent most of our time together; usually she talked and I listened. In spite of all her sorrows, she was able to detach herself from her own problems to be compassionate and understand my position. For that I loved her very much—as I still do. By the time Josette and I left Gourdon, Marceline was madly in love with a young man named Charly.

(Marceline's life has been a succession of peaks and valleys for many years. Today she is an accomplished cinematographer. She and her partner, who is also her companion, Joris Evens, have received worldwide acclaim. On one of my recent visits with her, Marceline told me, "I finally feel really and truly good.")

On my way home to Epinal I could not stop thinking about Marceline and what she gone through in camp. I had seen the deported people who returned, and I had heard all about the atrocities committed in concentration camps, but it wasn't until I spoke to Marceline that I accepted it as true: the gas chambers, the ovens, soap made out of human fat, gold dental work removed from the corpses' mouths, the women who were sexually abused by the German guards, all of it.

I began to visualize my own parents' deaths. Sometimes in my imagination they died in a gas chamber, choking; in another vision they were burned to ashes in the ovens. Papa had several gold caps, and I pictured him with spaces between his teeth, wearing the striped uniform in which he was just skin and bones like the people I had seen coming home at the Gare de l'Est. I just couldn't bear to think that my parents had suffered so. By what right was I spared? By what right had my life been so easy compared with theirs? In order to bear this heavy burden I would immerse myself in my old fantasies, imagining them in some small town in Russia to which they had escaped and where they were being cared for by some kind farmers. Someday they would write to me at Maman Marie's—at least one of them would.

When Josette and I reached Lyons, I had the urge to see the Lassalas family again, and so we detoured toward Clermont-Ferrand. They were happy to see us, and nothing there had changed. The villagers were also glad to see us, but were sorry to learn that my parents had not returned. Josette and I spent two wonderful weeks there. When I returned to Epinal, the affidavits necessary for an alien to obtain a visa for permanent residence in the United States had arrived. My father's family had sent them and had enclosed a letter insisting that we come to the States as soon as possible. Our lives from then on would be a fairy tale, they promised.

I was beginning to be skeptical about the glowing descriptions of what our lives were going to be like in the States. It was clear to me that Papa's family expected us to live at their home, yet my only desire was to be with Tante Regine. Although I was looking forward to meeting my other relatives, I had no intention of staying with them. In her letters, Tante Regine promised that Josette and I would remain at her home. I wrote to her immediately, insisting that I would come to the States only if we could live with her and asked her to explain this to Papa's sister, who obviously had the wrong impression.

In her next letter Tante Regine told me not to worry; Josette and I would remain with her. She had to ask Papa's family to make the affidavits for us because she could not afford to do so herself. In order to bring someone over from another country one had to prove that, if the emigrants were not able to support themselves, their benefactors, or sponsors, would be able to provide for them.

I was relieved; Tante Regine's explanation made sense. Maman had often made disparaging remarks about Papa's family, especially about the aunt who had sent our affidavits. Of the immediate family, Papa's oldest sister was the only one in a financial position to send the affidavits necessary for our visas. Her husband and their three sons ran a business; they manufactured women's clothing. I hardly remembered my aunt, but she and her family had visited my parents' home when I was quite young, and she had been somewhat unkind to Maman. Papa had another sister, who had never married, and two brothers, one of whom lived in Los Angeles. Most of them had visited our home at one time or another when I was very young, and I remembered them vaguely.

Maman's family consisted of Tante Regine, Tante Cecile, and several cousins in New York and Detroit, where Maman's uncle had settled many years before and had a large family of his own.

I was convinced by then that all these people should be able to contribute to the welfare of two orphans. I was eager to meet them and envisioned a pleasant life in America, the land of plenty, the young people's paradise. I sent a copy of the affidavits to the American embassy in Paris, applied for visas for Josette and me, and waited anxiously for a reply that never came. At the advice of my co-workers in the office, I sent the embassy a résumé that explained my desire to enter the States as soon as possible. Several weeks later I received an answer to that plea. The letter from the embassy stated that there were so many displaced people eager to emigrate to the United States that a waiting list had been established. When our file came up for review, they would indeed consider our application and get in touch with me at that time. I was sorely disappointed; I had expected that they would, upon receiving my résumé, send us our visas by return mail.

Epinal's Jewish community had shrunk considerably, but most of the Jewish families who had managed to survive had returned to try to pick up the pieces. They often invited Josette and me to their homes. I was too shy and too polite to refuse, but I hated to go, because I received too much, and not always the same, advice in each home. I began to feel like a Ping-Pong ball.

The Gertlers, who had received Josette in Limoges after I crossed the border, returned to Epinal periodically. Their home and stores had been completely destroyed during the bombing. They had to file many papers in order to receive compensation and apply for reconstruction. The paperwork necessitated their frequent trips to Epinal, although they had taken up residence in Paris.

Tante Regine could not understand why I hadn't succeeded in receiving a visa as yet, and she bombarded me with letters filled with advice. When I spoke of my frustrating dilemma to the Gertlers, they suggested that Josette and I come to Paris and stay with them until I obtained satisfaction from the American embassy. They were convinced that I was neglected only because I hadn't apeared in person to apply and that, if I went for the visas myself, we could leave for the States shortly. We would eat all our meals at their home but would sleep at a nearby hotel, since they said that their apartment was too small to accommodate us. I neded some time to tend to my affairs in Epinal, but I promised to take them up on their offer. Actually, the prospect of living in Paris was exciting. Paris was the city that Papa had taught me to love as he did. But before I could depart, I had to recoup and sell some of my parents' belongings that they had hidden with their friends.

Maman Marie had our dining room furniture, which I sold to a neighbor, and most of Maman's beautiful embroidered linens, pillows, and down comforters, which had been kept in a trunk all those years in the Collinses' attic, along with some fine china, crystal, and silver. I sold almost everything for a fraction of its value. At Gourdon, most of my parents' things had disappeared along with the Rosembergs'. Only a gold bracelet remained, along with some American dollars that we had buried on the grounds along with some of the Rosembergs' jewelry and money.

Some people denied having received any of my parents' belongings, and it was my word against theirs. I never would have known that our family car was hidden in the garage of one of my parents' friends if someone who worked for them had not mentioned it to Maman Marie. Cars were valuable, since all the cars built during the war were designed for the army. The price I received for the car was nowhere near its actual value, and it would not be an understatement to say that I was badly cheated. Selling the remainder of my parents' estate was distressing. It was to me an admission that they weren't coming back; if they did return, they certainly would be displeased to see that I had recovered a negligible amount of money compared with what they had put away. Most had been stolen or hidden from me and Josette.

Before I left for Paris Raymond and I called off our engagement. He was a gentleman and a gentle man.

I resigned from my job, and, until the last minute, Maman Marie and Papa Auguste tried to convince me to leave Josette with them, but I just couldn't, although I knew she would have been happy with them. Guiguite was engaged by then, and I promised to send the material for her wedding dress from the States.

Papa Auguste died several months later, leaving Maman Marie with her two foster children. (In addition to the numerous foster children Maman Marie raised, she harbored six Jewish children, including Josette and me.)

I left for Paris toward the end of September 1945. Maman Marie took us to the station. Her eyes were so blinded by tears that she fell and badly hurt her ankle. We all cried as we parted. The courageous woman waved to us from the platform, tears coursing down her cheeks.

Three hours later Josette and I were at the Gertlers' apartment. The Gertlers had three children: Jacques, Helene, and Rachel. Helene was two years older than I and was engaged to a medical student. An insufferable snob, she alone was not happy to see us. We had attended the same school in Epinal, and, although our parents had been good friends, we were not. (Helene had never had many friends.) She made our stay at their home uncomfortable, to say the least; from the moment we arrived I wished I were still among the Thiriets and the Collinses.

The rest of the Gertlers were cordial, but I sensed that they would be happy to see us leave as soon as possible. I was most uncomfortable and was short with Josette when she did not behave. I missed the warmth and the *laissez-aller* of my previous benefactors.

A day or two after our arrival, Josette and I went to the American embassy. To my surprise, there was a long line leading to the front door. We waited several hours, and it was closing time before we were admitted. The people at the head of the line had arrived as early as six o'clock, so I returned very early the next day. After waiting several hours I was finally admitted. The secretary I spoke to looked at my file and told me that my papers were in order and that I would be notified by mail when it was approved. I returned to the Gertlers' feeling discouraged. They agreed with me that it possibly would take some time before we could leave for the States. Helene remarked in a disapproving tone, "Are they going to have to stay here?" This question went through me like a knife and was answered by a very angry look from her father. That night in our dingy hotel, I cried myself to sleep.

I tried to spend as little time as possible in the Gertler home, so as not to be in the way. Josette and I walked all over Paris, our one pleasure in an otherwise depressing situation. I had money from the sale of my parents' belongings, and what I had recovered from Mrs. Rosemberg. It was not a great fortune, but it was enough to buy two tickets for the States and have some left over. The Gertlers were keeping it for me, which meant I had to ask

Mr. Gertler every time I needed pocket money. He always looked at me reproachfully on those occasions, as if I were taking his money. It became increasingly difficult for me to ask.

When it became clear that we were not going to the United States as soon as we had hoped, the Gertlers made arrangements (actually, Helene did all the leg work) for Josette and me to go to the suburbs of Paris, where a home had been opened to orphaned children of deported parents. The Gertlers didn't ask us; they told us to go.

We arrived at the home one cold, rainy day, and we stood in the hall waiting for the director to receive us. My heart sank. We had survived the dangers of the war years to end up in an orphanage once the danger was past! Children of all ages were running noisily everywhere. Josette and I clung to each other.

After what seemed a long time we were invited into the director's office. He questioned me about our background and showed absolutely no emotion on hearing my tale, which I admit, was not unique. All the children there as well as the young people on the staff were orphans or children of deported adults, or both. The director said that Josette would join the children in the home and that I would work in the office. When he introduced Josette to her group leader, she became hysterical and they had to take her away from me by force. That night, after the children were settled in their dormitory, I took my first meal with the staff. Josette's group leader suggested that I stay away from Josette for a while; the staff thought that she was too attached to me. I replied that we were there only temporarily, until we received our papers to go to the United States. That statement caused a few eyebrows to be raised. The home was sponsored by a left-wing organization, so my comment didn't go over very well. They called me *l'américaine* from then on, some in jest, others with disdain.

That same night, when everybody was ready to retire, I asked where I would sleep. They had forgotten all about me. Only the group leaders resided in the main house; the rest of the staff stayed in an adjoining house. I was led to a room devoid of furniture, except for a mattress on the floor. It was, thank goodness, clean. I later found out that staff members lived in the plainest of rooms, like cells in a monastery. Their purpose in being there was to care for the children, not to indulge themselves. The only persons who received a salary were the laundress, her helpers, the cook, and some cleaning help. Everyone else worked strictly on a volunteer basis.

That first night, alone in my spartan room, I thought that we had come to the end of the line. We would never get a visa to the United States. I was convinced by then that one had to know someone to get a visa. I thought, dejectedly, that I might as well forget about the States. But I certainly was not going to stay here. It was so unfair to Josette when she could be with Maman Marie, where she would be loved and well cared for. My hopes were shattered, and I decided I would leave the next day for Epinal.

The next morning at about six I was awakened by a young man of twenty, who brought in my suitcase. He was very cheerful and told me to hurry up and get dressed for staff breakfast. In the bright, sunny morning light, I noticed the beauty of my surroundings. The anxiety I had experienced the previous day had prevented my noticing much of anything.

When I entered the staff dining room for breakfast, everyone there was involved in a heated conversation and

[147]

paid no attention to me. I sat at their table, but I felt out of place. The young man who had brought me my suitcase winked at me. I wanted to know about Josette, but I didn't dare interrupt the discussion. After breakfast, everyone left except a pregnant woman in her middle thirties. By then I was so lost I wanted to die. I knew I was to work in the office, but in what capacity I didn't know. I didn't even know where the office was in that large house. The woman must have noticed my distress. She asked how I slept and then introduced herself as the director's wife. She was the house doctor, she said, but would give up her position when her baby was born. She questioned me about my background in a kind, soft tone. She seemed sympathetic and thought that we had come to the right place, where everyone was in the same predicament. She said, "Maybe you will learn to like it so much here that you won't want to leave for the United States." I didn't answer, but I knew I would leave one way or another. I told her I was worried about Josette, so she took me to the dormitory. The group leader told me that my sister was happily getting ready for breakfast and school and pointed out her bed to me. Josette had befriended the girl in the next bed and seemed contented. She proudly introduced me to her new friend. She felt superior; she had a big sister who worked here! The doctor came over and spoke kindly to Josette. As we walked to the office, she told me how beautiful Josette was and asked me to bring her to the dispensary for a medical checkup.

No one was in, and the office was a shambles when I finally found it. I waited for a while, hoping the director would arrive to tell me what he expected of me. I grew tired of waiting patiently after some time and decided to clean up the place. When the director showed up, much

[148]

later, he seemed pleased at what he saw and said he had forgotten all about me. In the office his attitude toward me was businesslike, with never a smile. But I saw a different side of him at dinner, when he was jovial and pleasant to the other staff members. He told me that I had been forced upon him by the main office in Pairs. He was genuinely puzzled when he learned that I wanted to go to the United States. He didn't have time to train temporary people, he told me. The fact that I had relatives in America didn't matter, he thought, because I hardly knew them. *This* was home to the orphan children of the deported. Everyone here, who worked for their welfare, was family. A large picture of Karl Marx hung on the wall. He told me that everyone working in the home was a socialist, which I decided was a polite name for a communist. A Jewish communist—what could be worse that that? The communists in France were not well thought of during the time I grew up. Calling someone a *sale communiste* (dirty communist) was like calling him the scum of the earth. Even so, there were more than a few communists in France.

Our conversation did not change my feelings about the place. After giving me a vague description of my duties, he handed me a book and said, "Read this." It was a translation of Karl Marx's *Das Kapital*.

The large house and grounds had been donated to the children by Josephine Baker, the beautiful and famous entertainer. A self-exiled black American who was married to Jo Bouillon, a noted orchestra leader, Miss Baker had adopted many, many children. The house was beautiful, avant-garde in architecture, with lots of glass and large rooms, which suited its present purpose well. The staff consisted of the director; his brother, who served as assistant director; the doctor; the group leaders, a young couple who openly lived together, a condition at that time shocking to me; three young men in their early twenties; and a woman in her thirties, who was Josette's leader. I made no friends among the younger staff members, but I was able to talk to the doctor. I was, however, more at ease with the cook, who was a Spanish refugee; the middle-aged laundress; her young helper; and, later on, Josette's leader. Eccentric in appearance, she looked much like a hippie of the sixties. She tried very hard to make a good communist of me, but by that time I had a new philosophy. If my parents were not to return, I had to conduct myself in a manner they would approve of. They were watching over me, I believed, so I couldn't do anything of which they would disapprove. (Maman Marie's beliefs had filtered through to me, after all!)

In addition to my work in the office, I helped out with the younger ones at bath time and bedtime. They all had an insatiable thirst for affection, so it was greatly rewarding to help them, even in such a small way. The children seemed as happy as children without parents could be. Everyone in a position of authority was kind to them. When the older ones misbehaved there were long talks with either the director or his assistant, or both, something like group therapy. There was a camaraderie in that house, where we all, adults and children, called one another by our first names. This in itself was something I was not used to. It was an informality quite unthinkable in most French circles.

Josette was contented. She had nice friends and went to school in the village every day with the other children. I was there when she needed me, and I tucked her into bed every night.

I was neither happy nor unhappy but simply impatient to get to the States.

[150]

Soon the new doctor came to take the place of the director's wife. He knew almost everybody and fit in well. Because he took a liking to me and I to him, he asked the director to let me help him during dispensary hours. I enjoyed my new duties and was honored that the doctor thought enough of me to let me help him. Many of the children were sick as a result of malnutrition or because of medical conditions that had been neglected during the war. Some of them had one parent; most had none. On visiting day we had to double our efforts to distract those children who had nobody to visit them.

Boys and girls slept in the same dormitory, and showers for staff and children were in one large room—another painful experience for me. There was no promiscuity in the house, just an open, communal way of life in which I was not comfortable.

I still corresponded with my old friends, and their letters kept me in touch with "my" world. I went to Paris regularly to see if any news had arrived from the embassy.

On my visits to Paris, Mrs. Gertler was kind and apologized that she couldn't keep us in her "small" apartment. (Actually, they had a large kitchen, three bedrooms, a large dining room, an even larger living room, and a foyer the size of a dance hall!) Financially, they were very well off. Maman Marie, in her minuscule house, found a way to shelter every stray she met, and so did the Lassalas family. But Mrs. Gertler really was kind; she simply did not have a voice in her household. I truly liked her. She once told me that she had made up her mind that if the Germans came to the house when she was there alone, she would tell them she was the maid. Well, one day they did come, and in her nervousness she kept saying, "I am my maid, I am my maid." As incredible as it seems, they believed her and left! (The Gertlers were one of the few families I knew who had no war casualties.) I resented the Gertlers because they had sent us to an orphanage. But it is true that when they asked us to come to Paris they had no idea that it would take so long to obtain our papers. They were not prepared to have two additional people in their household. Most people are compassionate; some are just able to give more of themselves. The Gertlers did lend Josette and me a helping hand, and for that I am grateful. Their son, Jacques, and daughter, Rachel, always made us feel at home, and I have fond memories of them.

Months passed, and I was losing hope of ever getting our papers. Tante Regine wrote letter after letter, telling me to write again to the embassy.

An epidemic of impetigo broke out in the home. Josette and a few other children were so badly infected they had to go to Paris for treatment at the Hôpital Saint-Louis. Josette had to be hospitalized for some time. I couldn't leave her, so the Gertlers put me up at a hotel. The day after Josette was admitted to the hospital, Mrs. Gertler and I went to visit her, bringing with us a small bouquet of violets. She was in a twenty-bed public ward. When I saw her, I gasped and stood in stunned silence for a moment, then I broke down in sobs. Mrs. Gertler tried to calm me, but she soon started to sob, too. The nurses had shaved off Josette's beautiful blonde curly hair. Her bald head was covered with bandages where the skin was badly infected. The sister in charge assured me that she would be all right; she explained that because of open wounds in Josette's scalp and the lice that had entered the lacerations, the shaved head was absolutely necessary. I visited Josette twice daily until she was discharged, and then we returned to the home.

More time elapsed, and I grew more impatient. On my

next day off I returned to the embassy, and took Josette with me.

The line had already formed and extended around the corner. It was a cold, rainy day, but we waited and were finally admitted hours later. I received the same polite answer from the receptionist: "As soon as your file is reviewed . . . Please be patient." I was tired, and Josette was exhausted. It wasn't easy for a child of six to stand in line for hours. We were wet and hungry. I was discouraged and felt as if I had hit bottom. I started to break down. Josette implored me not to cry. But then she, too, started to sob. We must have been some sight, standing there in the lobby, wet, hungry, and crying on each other's shoulders. We attracted the attention of a man who questioned us and tried to console us, but we simply couldn't stop crying. He managed to get me to tell him about my problem and about how frustrated I was at being rejected each time I came to the embassy. He listened without interrupting. When I had finished, he asked for our names and some other information, which he jotted down on a piece of paper. Then he asked us to wait there for him. I then realized he spoke perfect French, but with a thick American accent. When I calmed down, I was rather ashamed of my display of emotion and started to leave, but the man, now carrying his coat, caught up with us as we reached the door.

He took Josette by the hand, and we walked a few blocks to Harry's American Bar, a hangout quite popular with Americans then and now. The gentleman bought us some sandwiches and hot chocolate. "Eat and relax; everything will be all right," he said. By then I was calmer and had lost my nerve. What was I doing in that noisy place, surrounded by jolly people who only spoke English. Our new friend was a distinguished-looking, white-haired American in his sixties. I never forget a face, but names do escape me, and, to my sorrow, his is no exception. He was kind to both of us and, after we finished our meal, made us promise to return the following morning at nine. He was staying at the Hotel Crillon, directly across the street from the embassy, and he would meet us at the embassy door; there would be no need for us to stay in line. When he left us, I remember him saying, "Take *la petite fille* home; rest and stop worrying. Your troubles are over." He asked if we had enough money. When I assured him that we did, he bade us good day and left.

I stood there holding Josette's hand, not knowing exactly what to expect the next day, but suspecting that we had finally met the influential person we had been dreaming of. When we got back to the Gertlers' home, I told them what had happened. They looked at me as if I were crazy, making up a tale like that, but Josette told them, *"C'est vrai, c'est vrai,"* and they were as amazed as I had been. They concluded that our new friend must be a wealthy man if he stayed at the Crillon, one of the most expensive hotels in Paris. I could not sleep all night, and at seven the next morning Josette and I were in front of the embassy door.

At precisely nine the gentleman tapped me on the shoulder. We followed him inside, walking past several offices. Everyone greeted him deferentially. We reached the office of the vice-consul in charge of emigration, where a secretary received us and escorted us into a large office. I had never seen anything so grand in my life, not even at the Chaumettes' home. My knees were shaking, my legs felt like cotton, and my heart was pounding so hard that I thought I would faint. A large man seated behind a desk asked us to sit down. Our friend spoke to him briefly in English and then told me that this man would help us with our papers. He said we were to ask for him at the reception desk on our way out.

The vice-consul, unlike our friend, was stern and businesslike. Our file was on the desk in front of him. He flipped through the pages without so much as a glance at us. Without a doubt, this man held our future in his hands. He picked up the phone and spoke briefly. Because he spoke English, I could not understand what he said. Only then did he address me in French. He read my résumé, questioned me about it, and shook his head incredulously. His secretary brought in some papers, which he signed. Josette was silent and still. I think she understood that something important was taking place. He placed all the papers in an envelope, and finally he spoke: "As a servant of the United States Government, it is my pleasure and privilege to grant you admission to the United States of America as permanent residents. I think you will be an asset to your new country, and no doubt you will become fine citizens." He handed me the large envelope, shook my hand, tapped Josette's head, and wished us both good luck. I was afraid to believe we finally had our visas. It was too good to be true.

We asked for our benefactor when we reached the reception desk, and he came out to greet us. I showed him the envelope, and he looked at its contents and said, "Well, your worries are over; you finally have your visas." I didn't know how to thank him. I told him I wanted to do something for him, but he only seemed amused. I insisted, so he told me that he would be positively thrilled if I could just get him some endive, because he adored it and could never get any in his hotel dining room. As strange as this request may seem, that is what he asked for! I thank him again and again, and he said, "I have two sisters back home in Saint Louis, and I hope if they are

ever in need, someone will give them a helping hand."
After bidding him good-bye, we went straight to the
Gertlers' home. If they ever doubted my story, the papers
now spoke for themselves. I recall that I was so afraid of
losing the envelope that I held it with both hands and
made Josette hold on to my coat.

I had not realized that endive was so scarce. I went to
every vegetable store in Paris, it seemed. When finally I
found some, I bought as much as I could. There were no
shopping bags in France at the time, so the grocer
wrapped the endive in newspapers. Josette and I must
have been a comical sight, walking into the elegant embassy with an armful of newspaper-wrapped endive. Our
friend was truly embarrassed, but obviously touched by
our gratitude. I guess he didn't think I would ever find
any and so felt safe in asking for it. Nevertheless, he
thanked me warmly and wished us much good luck. I
never did find out what our friend's position was at the
embassy.

The Gertlers and I thought we would leave shortly, but
when I went to inquire about passage on a boat, I received a big surprise. The war was just over; transatlantic
transportation had not resumed its regular schedule, and
it would be some time before it would. All the ships
available were booked at least six months in advance. I
put our names on a long list and returned, discouraged, to
the orphan home. The staff was not at all impressed by
my good fortune, and some were actually annoyed that I
was so unhappy about not obtaining immediate transportation. They were proud of their work at the home and
were totally dedicated to the children, so it disappointed
them that they had been unsuccessful in persuading me
to stay where they believed Josette and I belonged. Sub-
sequently, their attitude became one of total indifference.

The director's wife, who lived at the home with her new baby, still showed me some kindness, but I sensed that she, too, was disappointed in me.

Actually, the new doctor made my stay bearable. By that time I worked full-time for him, and he was extremely pleased with my efforts. He insisted that I was an asset to the home, that I had the gift of being able to give of myself effortlessly. This quality, he told me, was something much needed in the work of the home. Furthermore, he was concerned for me, because he thought that my expectations of our future life in the United States were far too high. No matter how nice my relatives were, they could never meet the standards I had set. He was certain I would be quite disappointed and perhaps traumatized psychologically by what surely awaited me. He assured me that if we remained in France he would personally see to it that Josette and I received all the advantages to which war orphans were entitled. He would make sure that I furthered my education in any field for which I was suited.

The doctor was more than old enough to be my father, but by that time I was secretly in love with him. He reminded me of Papa: he had blue eyes and the same ability to talk to anyone of any age or intellectual capacity. The children were crazy about him and used to fake illness just to have an excuse to visit the infirmary. He had unlimited patience and love, and everyone he touched walked away feeling better. I believe that I performed well only because of his example, which was contagious. But in spite of all his long talks with me, I was still determined to go to the States.

Tante Regine bombarded me with letters full of advice on how to precipitate our departure; every letter was filled with promises of a better life. I kept remembering how much I had loved Tante Regine as a child and the love she had given me. I suppose that I was looking for a substitute mother. Josette and I would live with her, and I couldn't wait for our departure.

Mr. Gertler had a brilliant idea: we should go to America by plane. We had enough money to pay for two one-way tickets. That idea was exciting, because in 1946 flying was strictly for VIPs. Most people, no matter how wealthy, traveled by car, train, or ship. Airplanes were for the air force and a few privileged civilians. The following day we went to the TWA office and were told that there was no space available. Few planes were in service, and the best they could do was to put us on a standby list. They told me to stay in the house every day until five o'clock in case the clerk called us with news of available space.

The Gertlers had no phone. This wasn't uncommon in those years, and new phone service was unobtainable regardless of one's financial status. Therefore, we had to rely on the phone at the hotel. The Gertlers lived nearby, but I could not expect anyone from the hotel to call for me there. (They lived on the fifth floor, but even their luxury apartment building had no elevator.) So, during the day we spent most of our time in the hotel and took our evening meals with the Gertlers. It was a very trying period. I read a lot, but Josette was restless, and I must admit that I was often impatient with her. Then I would feel guilty, as always. Josette was everything to me. She was the last tangible link to my parents. I took their last wish very seriously. Josette was my responsibility, and everything I did was done with her welfare in mind. Because I was young, my decisions may not always have been the best ones, but things had turned out well thus far.

On weekends we took long walks all over Paris, the Paris Papa loved so much. I took Josette with me everywhere, to the Zoo de Vincennes, to Luna Park on a *bateau mouche*, to the Bois de Boulogne. My favorite place was the Champs-Elysées. Papa used to say that when one sat at a sidewalk café on the Champs-Elysées, one could smell the perfume of the elegant women passing by. So, with Josette, I spent many Sunday afternoons at cafés.

I was still overwhelmed by the beauty of the city, and I wondered then whether New York would be as beautiful.

Several weeks went by, and Josette became very ill. The doctor came to the hotel several times. She had acute bronchitis and a high fever. The hotel was poorly heated, when it was heated at all. I hardly ever left the room. Mrs. Gertler sent food with Rachel, who occasionally stayed with Josette so that I could get some fresh air. Josette's condition was not improving. The doctor kept changing the medicine, to no avail. Her temperature remained high, and I was worried. Antibiotics were not in use in those days, so any infectious illness was potentially serious or even fatal. I was concerned that we might get a call from the airlines and be unable to leave. We might miss our chance. Many weeks later, fortunately, Josette's condition improved, and we were once again able to go out.

I was more impatient than ever, and I pestered the airline agents, who assured me that they would call us as soon as space was available. Mr. Gertler suggested that I go to the embassy and ask my benefactor to pull some strings at the airlines, but I simply could not impose further. Two weeks later, when I thought I could wait no longer, I was just about to leave the hotel when someone told me I was wanted on the phone. It was the airlines! Two seats were available that very midnight on a flight departing from Orly. I sent telegrams to the Collinses, the Thiriets, the Lassalas, the Rosembergs, and Tante Regine.

Mr. Gertler took us to the airport, where the plane—a converted army aircraft—awaited its passengers. With some amazement, I noticed that it was more than half empty on takeoff. On board we were served only chewing gum and chocolate bars. Our first stop was at Shannon, where we ate a small meal, which to us seemed lavish after our years of simple fare. We didn't know what to eat first. Our next stop was Gander, Newfoundland, where we ate again, even more sumptuously than we had in Ireland, since there was no food shortage in Gander. The food was actually very ordinary: eggs, bacon, rolls, butter, jelly, home fries, and danishes. We might take such a breakfast for granted now, but to Josette and me it seemed like a meal fit for a king. Such basic foods were still luxuries in postwar France.

Josette slept through a good part of the trip. No one else on board spoke French, so I was left alone with my own thoughts. It was an exhilarating few hours. My anticipation of a new life was blown completely out of proportion. I felt suspended between two worlds. In one I had left the sadness of my past, but I left France with regrets because it was, after all, my home. In the other world— the United States—I was sure nothing would ever hurt us again. I was euphoric. For several years afterward, whenever I spotted an airplane flying overhead, I would think of my flight as one of the happiest times in my life. To this day, on receiving good tidings I am glad, but I never anticipate anything until it actually happens, for fear of being disappointed.

On April 15, 1946, Josette and I landed at La Guardia Airport. It was the first night of Passover.

[160]

PART III

When I decided to write about my wartime and postwar experiences, I firmly intended to end the story at the point of our arrival in New York. Until now, I thought I'd rather choke on the words than tell anyone what we faced when we came to the United States, to the bosom of our family. It occurred to me, however, that if I didn't write a conclusion, the reader might simply assume that Josette and I lived happily ever after. Alas, there is only one Cinderella, and her story is a fairy tale. Sometimes I think that the four years following the war were more destructive to our emotional well-being than all our years of hiding.

I don't recall the exact time we landed at La Guardia, but I do recall that the sun was setting.

The terminal, a large, bare hangar, was anything but the comfortable place today's terminals are. I soon heard someone calling my name. It was Tante Regine! We ran to greet each other and kissed through the wire fence that separated passengers from others. I still remember what I felt then: though our parents had not come back, Josette and I had Tante Regine now, and all would be well.

It seemed like hours before we were cleared through customs; by the time we were allowed to meet our other relatives, it was dark. We ran to Tante Regine and cried as we embraced each other warmly. Finally, she introduced us to Papa's oldest sister, her husband, and their son, who was twenty years older than I. The only way we could communicate with them was in Yiddish. Although I had never learned Yiddish, it is derived from German, and, after four years of occupation, I spoke and understood German well.

From her letters, I knew that Tante Regine, then in her late thirties, had recently been married for the first time. Her husband had just been discharged from the army, and she was working to help support them. Her letters had led me to believe that Josette and I would live with her; she also wrote that she had moved to a larger apartment—at great expense, she often reminded me—so that we could have our own room. Therefore, it came as a rude shock when, as we were leaving, Tante Regine took me aside and informed me that Josette and I were to go home with Papa's relatives. She might as well have exploded a bomb in my face.

Why had she written about her arrangements for us if she had no intention of keeping us? My reluctance to emigrate to the United States had been worn away by all her promises; she had finally succeeded in convincing me that Josette and I were bound for the Garden of Eden. In spite of our emotional suffering, it had been impossible for me, adolescent as I was, to be realistic; I persisted in believing that everything would be all right at the end of the rainbow—which I was certain to reach. Well, I had reached the rainbow's end—and the end of my fantasies.

As we left the terminal, Tante Regine explained that our paternal relatives had, after all, sent us the affidavits; they were wealthy and would take good care of us. It wouldn't be nice to hurt their feelings, she said, and anyway, she would see us often. My heart sank. I couldn't believe what I was hearing. It was only the first of many disappointments, but it was hard to accept. In the years that followed, I realized that Tante Regine was not at that time in a position, emotionally or financially, to undertake the responsibility of caring for two orphans. Neither was Tante Cecile. What I objected to most, though, was that I had been misinformed.

I suppose that in her heart Tante Regine thought we would be better off in America than in France. Our coming was a way to forestall or prevent me from entering into a marriage she didn't approve of. Actually, her strategy had worked. Had I known this, I would never have agreed to expatriate. I didn't understand it at the time, but this unfortunate turn of events had taught me a great lesson, and I eventually learned that out of every bad experience one gains wisdom. As the French say, "*Après la pluie, le beaux temps*" (after the storm, the sunshine).

Our good-byes to Tante Regine were strained. She promised to visit us soon.

We finally arrived at my aunt's home in the Bronx. The apartment was crowded with friends and relatives who had come to celebrate the first night of Passover. The table was set in the tremendous dining room. And after lengthy introductions, we were finally permitted to

[163]

be seated and partake in the festivities. The rituals seemed strange to us; we had been raised in a nonpracticing French Jewish home.

It was by then very late. Not only were we exhausted from our long voyage, but I was nauseated and longed for a cozy bed. Any bed! Instead we were surrounded by loud voices speaking an unfamiliar language. Strangers stared at us as if we had just arrived from outer space.

Our relatives asked no questions whatsoever. I was utterly baffled by what seemed to be their total indifference. They didn't want to know any details, horrible or not. The questions came mostly from curious friends, and in most cases my answers were met with incredulity. The remark that silenced me was this: "Oh, Jacqueline, you have a very vivid imagination!" I was so stunned by this response that I resolved at that moment never to talk about the war years again or about the impact they had had on Josette and me. Thereafter, I replied to questions by saying, "Oh, it's a long story. I don't want to bore you." And I buried deep within me all the hurt and tried hard to forget. Even I knew that the past, however terrible, must not be dwelled upon.

I was in a state of shock, completely out of my element. As the evening progressed, my stomach grew queasier, but I was too shy to ask to be excused. I was alone among cackling strangers who by now were involved in their own private and animated conversations, which made us feel even more detached.

I soon had what I believed to be my first severe migraine headache. The situation became intolerable, and I truly wanted to die. I clearly remember that I felt what might be called "high," as if my feet were not touching the ground—a leftover from the long and bumpy flight from Newfoundland to New York.

When Josette finally fell asleep at the table, our relatives, who seemed to have forgotten we were there, realized we needed rest. We were shown to our room. Our bedroom seemed to be a converted pantry, located off the kitchen. It did have one small window that overlooked a dark courtyard. Its sparse furnishings consisted of a chair, a cupboard for our clothes, and a makeshift bed that Josette and I had to share. It was too small for one, let alone two, people. The mattress was actually three pillows that belonged to a now defunct couch. The only light was an unshaded bulb in the ceiling form which a cord hung that one had to pull in order to turn the light on or off. I clearly recall thinking that I had never seen that in my native France where lights always had switches.

I had been told in so many letters that Josette and I would be treated like princesses in the United States. If this room was any indication of how American princesses lived, I wondered, with dismay, what the future held in store.

The room seemed even shabbier in contrast to the otherwise lavishly furnished home.

In spite of the narrowness of the bed and the discomfort, Josette eventually fell asleep. I cried until I was cried out.

Josette and I remained at my aunt's home where she and her family constantly reminded me that it was Maman's fault that my parents had not come to America. They always and often referred to Maman unkindly. They did not even speak of Papa with love. If it were not for Papa's love for France and French wine, my aunt said, then Papa and Maman would be alive. My father never drank alcoholic beverages except an occasional glass of beer on a hot summer day, and this kind of talk hurt me deeply and reinforced my first impression of my aunt. At the airport, my aunt had caused me to bristle by saying, "Thank God, Josette and Jacqueline will never again have to sleep in a Gentile home." How dare she? Gentiles had saved our lives. I considered her remark unforgivable. It was racism in reverse, but I never argued with them. I soon understood what the doctor in the French home had tried to tell me. How could these people understand? Pain is something that cannot be described adequately or understood fully, except by someone who has experienced it. No one in that household ever questioned me about how we survived the four years after my parents were deported, nor did they ask how Papa and Maman were arrested. But they told me constantly about the deprivations they had to endure during the war, such as the shortage of cigarettes, nylon stockings, and sugar. Although I kept silent, this irritated me. Compared to what the Europeans had had to do without, theirs were petty complaints.

I celebrated my eighteenth birthday two weeks after we arrived in the States. I was older than my years in some respects, but I lacked the insight necessary to understand my aunt and her family. I needed understanding, and Josette and I both needed love. As far as they were concerned, the fact that they brought us to America was sufficient and was a gesture worthy of our complete gratitude.

Several days passed. With my fluent German as a base, I could communicate quite well in Yiddish with my aunt and with the rest of the family. When they didn't speak English, I was able to feel that I was a part of the household. It was much harder for Josette, who was glued to me. She seemed so scared that she reverted to an almost infantile stage and asked me to carry her. My relatives scolded me for giving in and "babying" her. I responded, "She needs love and affection," and they raised their eyebrows and shoulders disapprovingly.

A few days after our arrival, my aunt, Josette, and I went shopping for groceries. My aunt was stopped by a man she knew, and after all the proper introductions the man said in Yiddish, "She is a good-looking young girl. She will soon have a boyfriend." My aunt replied, "She has a boyfriend. She is engaged and will soon be married." I was absolutely taken aback by this statement and thought perhaps I had misunderstood. I kept quiet until we reached her home, and frankly I don't know how I found the courage to overcome my crippling shyness and question my aunt.

I was a little bit afraid of her. My aunt was a domineering woman. In the brief time I had been there, I had observed that she led the whole family by the nose, including her daughters-in-law and certainly her sons, especially her unmarried thirty-eight-year-old son, who was a classic mama's boy.

But I did find the courage, and I learned that I had not misunderstood her statement. The family had brought me over from France to marry my cousin! I called Tante Regine and babbled to her, in a state of hysteria for the first time since my parents were arrested. "Don't be foolish, Jacqueline," she calmly answered. "He is rich and he will take good care of you and Josette. You can learn to love a man if he is good to you."

I wept, "But I'm barely eighteen. I want to be in love when I marry."

Suddenly, I realized that Tante Regine wanted no part of Josette and me. My story had not surprised her. She had been in on these plans from the start. I should have been more suspicious, because my cousin didn't treat me

[167]

as an older cousin usually treats a kid. He behaved more like a prospective suitor. I had not wanted to acknowledge this even to myself, but it became obvious to me, on looking back on the days since our arrival, that everyone in the family saw me as the prospective bride for the last unmarried man in the family.

He started to take me out nightly and ordered his sisters-in-law to take me shopping for clothes. Before long, he began to dictate what I should wear.

He was a nondescript man—slim, of medium height, and slightly balding. Because he seemed ancient to me and because he was my first cousin, I was disinclined to feel romantic toward him.

Every time I saw a plane flying overhead I wished I were on it. The many hours I had spent suspended between the two worlds were filled with pleasant anticipation of a happiness that never materialized. I kept hoping that my present state of affairs was just a dream and that I would wake up in the plane on my way to a better life.

Tante Cecile, Uncle Albert, and Jeannine finally came to visit us at our aunt's home, a little late perhaps, but I soon forgot that when I saw their familiar faces. I was so happy to speak French once again. Tante Cecile admitted that she had advised her sister Regine to leave us in France, since neither of them was equipped to care for two kids. She agreed that the trickery involved in getting us to the States was extremely unfair, and she begged me not to enter a prearranged marriage without careful consideration.

According to Tante Cecile, Tante Regine believed that marrying me off to a rich man—a cousin or otherwise—would solve all my problems, ease her conscience, and above all absolve her of any responsibilities. This conversation gave me hope and courage.

Three months had elapsed since we had arrived at my aunt's home, where life for me was no longer bearable. It was hard to believe I had come so far for this. I had been so misled. I certainly didn't feel like a princess, but more like a creature at a farm auction.

I reasoned that if Josette and I could survive a war, we could survive anything. "I am only eighteen. I will not marry a man twenty years my senior; when I do marry, it will be for love," I vowed.

So one morning, I packed our suitcases and called Tante Regine. I told her I had decided to go to the French embassy and request to be repatriated. I would rather go back to the home with Josette or to Maman Marie, who would be delighted to have Josette back. As orphans of war, we were entitled to many benefits from the government, and I could pursue my education. The thought of returning to France and seeing my kind friends filled me with new hope. Tante Regine quieted me, however, and asked me to come to her home with Josette.

My aunt was shocked when I announced that we were leaving and told her why. But when she recovered her composure, her parting words were cutting. She wasn't surprised by my behavior, she said. I took after my mother. This last statement reinforced my feelings and convinced me that I had made the right decision.

We took the subway, suitcases and all, got lost, and ended up somewhere in Brooklyn.

Late that Friday evening we finally arrived in Forest Hills to a worried Tante Regine. The following Monday I began working in a perfume factory, and Josette, who had hardly been out of my sight since the day I picked her up in Arles, went to an orphanage sponsored by a Jewish organization, the Shield of David.

I think that the most psychologically destructive event in both our lives was Josette's being placed in the orphanage. For Josette, being separated from me was traumatic. As for me, I felt that I had betrayed my parents' wish. I remembered their last words to me: "Take care of Josette." I had so far, but now I had failed.

I visited Josette whenever my job would allow. She cried each time I left, and each time, the guilt within me mounted to a dangerous level. I felt more like a mother who had abandoned her child than a sister who had done the only thing she could do.

I worked in a French cosmetic factory for a year. It was Tante Regine's choice mostly because many of the workers spoke French. It was not a happy year. Most of the French women I met were war brides from World War I. They were, of course, much older than I and had been completely assimilated into the American way of life.

I washed perfume bottles on an assembly line, but I was later promoted to labeling and packing the bottles. The fast-moving line was supervised by a French woman with a critical eye and a disposition to match. She seemed more like a jail warden than a co-worker, and she pulled rank on us often and with great enjoyment. She had her pets; I was not one of them. I soon found out that my being Jewish was the reason for the unfounded and obvious dislike for me.

After work I ate a light dinner and then attended evening classes in English at the old Central Commercial High School on East Forty-second Street. I still treasure the diploma I received when I graduated.

I got back to Tante Regine's home around 11:15 P.M. and went immediately to bed, as I had to be at work by eight in the morning. Most of the time Tante Regine was already asleep, because she too had to rise early to go to work.

Saturdays I cleaned my room and did the laundry. Sundays I rose very early to take a long subway ride to the orphanage in the Hunts Point section of the Bronx to take Josette out for the day.

We usually went to a movie and ate out or took walks in the park, weather permitting. A woman not especially fond of children, Tante Regine preferred that Josette not spend weekends at her home.

Sunday was our favorite day of the week, because Josette and I were together. I bought her pretty dresses out of my meager salary of twenty-three dollars a week. Josette would cry bitterly every time I left. I was always depressed during the ride back to Forest Hills. I never complained to Tante Regine; it was useless. Obviously I started to resent her, however, and held her responsible for our ill fate.

Josette was so unhappy at the home that one Sunday I took her to my father's family and begged them to take Josette back. They flatly refused, claiming that I should have given the matter some thought before I showed so much independence, and they blamed Tante Regine for the outcome. We left with our heads down and without hope—never to communicate with that part of our family again.

Josette returned to the home, and my life continued much in the same manner for another year.

I made some friends at work, but I was so busy with school and visiting Josette on Sundays and holidays that I didn't have much time to socialize. Tante Regine was not unkind, nor was Uncle Benno, but she hadn't bargained for my presence in her home, and she was no longer the

Tante Regine I once knew. The hard life she had experienced in the United States had greatly embittered her. She showed me no love or affection and was critical of my every move. My increasing shyness and low self-esteem stunted my emotional growth. My only comforts were my visits to the orphanage and my fantasies that a letter would come from France announcing my parents' return.

I worked patiently at the factory for a year, since I couldn't afford to quit until my paid, two-week vacation, when I went out to look for a job. I was hired as a receptionist at a beauty parlor in midtown Manhattan, where I remained for several months. It was quite an improvement, and I enjoyed my work and co-workers immensely. All was well until my boss started to make unwanted passes at me. I declined his advances and left shortly thereafter. I applied for a job in nearby Gimbels department store, and I worked there for quite a while.

It was about that time that I left Tante Regine's home, where I felt unwanted, for a furnished room near Riverside Drive. It had been recommended by Ginette, a French girl I knew, who resided there with her brother. They too had lost their parents in a concentration camp and had come to relatives who had promised them the world in their letters. Like us, Ginette and her brother came and were disappointed at their reception. They were somewhat older than I, and their aim was to work and save until they could accumulate enough money to return to their beloved France. They eventually did just that.

Ginette and I became like sisters. It was good to have a friend again! She would often join me on my visits to the orphanage, and we would take Josette home on weekends. There was a community kitchen where we could cook our meals, and on weekends I enjoyed cooking meals "à la française" for all of us.

I was always broke. The fifteen-dollar rent was to be paid weekly, and I earned only about twenty-seven dollars. I was forever borrowing money from my co-workers, whom I would repay on payday and borrow again at midweek until the following payday. Somehow I always managed to shower Josette with little gifts. But with my precarious financial situation, what I missed most of all was being able to buy clothing. I always liked to look nice, so it was difficult to work in a department store where I saw clothing on display but could not purchase anything.

I soon befriended a young girl at work, Ruth. She came from a wealthy family and worked part-time only to occupy herself. She was not college material, and she was working, she said, until she found a husband. Ruth was attractive and always well dressed. She obviously noticed my limited wardrobe, and one day she came to work with bags full of clothes for me. I was a little humiliated, but secretly quite happy at my good fortune. I couldn't wait to get back to my room and look through everything. Unfortunately, every one of the beautiful garments was too small! But a *débrouillarde* remains a *débrouillarde*, so I opened seams and hems and ended up with an extensive wardrobe such as I had never dreamed of owning.

It was a little embarrassing to go to work wearing Ruth's discarded clothes, but she was a good friend and never mentioned it.

Wealthy people from South America often came to New York to shop, many of them at Gimbels. Most of them spoke perfect French but little English. I was often summoned to help them shop throughout the store.

On one occasion a pilot from Air France came to the

store. I was called upon to translate for him. Being my countryman and old enough to be my father, he took a special interest in me. During his frequent stops in New York he visited me at the store and brought me magazines and little goodies. During one of his stopovers he suggested that I apply for job at Air France, where he would put in a good word for me.

The personnel department interviewer at Air France commented that I seemed intelligent but that I couldn't type—a requirement for that job. I replied that I was nervous because he was looking over my shoulder as I typed. (I had never typed in my life.) I asked that he give me a chance at the job and said I would work for two weeks without pay. I vowed I would prove myself worthy of it. I got the job.

That night I borrowed an old typewriter from a friend, bought a book on typing, and practiced every night until the wee hours in my small furnished room. I was almost evicted because the clacking of the keys disturbed my neighbors. Some weeks later I was able to type—albeit in an unorthodox manner.

By the time I joined Air France, my English had improved a great deal. I was taking night courses for advanced foreigners at Hunter College. When I applied, I recall that the sixty-dollar fee per credit was a phenomenal amount, which set me back even further. But I was determined to better myself and to speak English correctly. Papa's remarks about the power of education had left their mark.

Working for Air France brought me back to an almost totally French environment, and it made me more keenly aware of my parents' absence than ever. All my French friends had parents. I was often invited to their homes, but seeing them in a normal family environment made my lack of immediate family all the more painful, so I began inventing excuses each time I was invited. I spent most of my spare time with Josette and Ginette.

Two years after I began working at Air France and shortly before I was to return to France with Josette—in all probability to marry Raymond, with whom I had been corresponding—I met, fell in love with, and married Jonas Wolf. In the twenty-nine years of our marriage, we have been blessed with two wonderful children, Paul and Michele.

When I announced that I was getting married, Josette was sick with fear at the idea she was losing me, though she soon realized that Jonas was no threat to her relationship with me. When my son Paul was born, Josette's life rapidly found a new focus; he became her pet, the center of her life. By the time Michele was born, Josette was a young lady of twenty-one. A year later she married Philip, a very special man.

History should teach us to go on, to seek a better way of life. Yet the horror of war threatens us always. When the war in Europe ended, I asked myself over and over why the world had allowed it to happen at all. When I arrived in the United States, I intended to start an entirely new life, but I prayed that my parents' suffering and death were not in vain, that the world had learned a lesson. I was sure that the murder of so many millions of people would serve as a constant reminder of man's inhumanity to man. I was wrong.

The ink on the armistice papers was barely dry when the United States and Russia entered into the cold war. This saddened and infuriated me. Racism was rampant;

religious intolerance was just as apparent. I had hoped I would never be hurt again because of my religious heritage. To questions about my religion, I still answer that I am a human being.

Jewish people are supposed to believe that chicken soup heals better than antibiotics. As the proud grandmother of a little girl named Lauren Beth, aged five, I can say that she is better for me than chicken soup—any time. When she appears at my door after a few days' absence, my life is filled with joy. Through her and the grandchildren to come, my parents will live on. Hitler, abominable man, lost because, against all odds, I and many others were saved. My children were born, and Lauren Beth was born, and they are here to keep the memory alive. We will go on, we will multiply, and we will bring forth more Prousts, Chagalls, Einsteins, and Bernhardts. Above all, we will contribute as we have in the past to make the world a better place in which to live.

EPILOGUE

I have just read Helen Epstein's book, *Children of the Holocaust*. Ms. Epstein interviewed children of people who survived terms in concentration camps. I am overwhelmed by her ability to express and analyze feelings that we all share—feelings that I have been unable to express even to myself until now. In one instance, Ms. Epstein relates an experience her mother had after being freed by the Allies. The young woman returned home and was invited to dinner at the home of one of her mother's friends, a woman who had been entrusted with some of the family's most valuable belongings. The hostess served dinner at a table set with the young woman's own mother's best linens, china, and sterling. Strangely enough, the young woman felt embarrassed instead of angry. I, too, was served dinner on Maman's best Limoges by "friends" of my parents. I, too, felt embarrassment instead of anger—embarrassment for people so unfeeling.

The book also helped me to understand the people I met here who told me I had a vivid imagination and then turned their backs on me. How could they possibly understand? Most of us dismiss what we don't understand.

Most of the people interviewed in *Children of the Holocaust* achieved the goals they set for themselves. Unfortunately, I feel that I did not. Papa placed such emphasis on education and culture. As a child I don't recall ever being given a doll; Papa's presents were always books. I always worried about my marks in school and was always concerned that I would not live up to Papa's high expectations. When my son was old enough to understand, I, too, stressed education; a born student, he didn't need any encouragement, and I needn't have worried. Papa would have been very proud of him. When my daughter was born, I resolved to take great interest in her schooling, but I recalled the pressures of my own school years and decided to let her move at her own pace, at which she has managed very well.

Madison Avenue would have us believe that the American way of life cannot be improved upon. It was more than a little difficult for me when I arrived from the chaotic world I had known not to feel insecure when confronted with what I immediately perceived as the *only* American way. For years I suffered in my attempts to be perfect so that people here would like me. I was determined to be loved by everyone.

In spite of my inner conflicts, I was, after many years, able to make sense of my life. Having to care for Josette and, later, my own family probably stabilized me. I know myself to be a giver who derives great joy in doing for others, and I know this prevented me many times from dwelling on my own problems. Nevertheless, the eruptions occur; while I haven't found a cure for them, I understand why they happen, just how much I have repressed, and that I can't be perfect.

The compulsion that motivated me to write this book wasn't immediately clear to me even when the book was finished. I kept reading those pages over and over again. Something was missing. My apparent guilt toward Josette was not a revelation; I had been aware of it for many years. What was I afraid of? What was I searching for? There were moments as I was writing when I actually felt as if I had been transported back in time to 18 Rue des Minimes and my parents' kitchen, where the family often gathered around the large round table. It was always winter, and every detail in the room became crystal clear. I could feel the warmth of the coal fire nearby and see the rooftops of Epinal through the steam-covered window. Only the wallpaper remained blurred; this would distract me, and I would try hard to recall its design, but in vain. As I came back to reality, I always felt empty and sad. I kept reading, yet each time I neared the end, I felt that some pieces of the puzzle were missing. The dissatisfaction haunted me.

Then it occurred to me that I was afraid to discover something most displeasing. The truth surfaced: I had not lived up to my parents' expectations or to their standards. I was a failure! After all, I was supposed to be the first woman lawyer in the family, according to Papa. And in other areas I hadn't lived up to Maman's standards either. I was a failure!

In France most of the women in my family had great careers. Jeannine became a successful businesswoman,

Ida was decorated by the president himself for her invaluable contributions in the arts; Marceline is a widely recognized cinematographer, and Jacqueline is her private secretary and right hand. They are all self-made women.

I had remained convinced all these years that my parents—who, I believed, could see me at all times—were disappointed in me. But from the time they were cruelly taken away from me, I had channeled all my energies toward survival, leaving little time for recreation, sports, or intellectual growth. At least I thought so, but on looking back, I realize how much I accomplished. I read avidly and went to night school to perfect my English. I built furniture I couldn't afford to buy; recycling was my forte before it became stylish. I learned to sew and knit clothes for my children and was more often than not complimented on my cooking. No matter how poor we were, our home always reflected a sense of beauty.

How I tortured myself all these years, thinking so little of myself because I had not lived up to an image drawn so long ago. I no longer feel guilty about my past; perhaps I even feel a little proud. The guilt belongs to those who created the awful circumstances for the Josettes and Jacquelines and to those who closed their eyes when they could have helped.

I often think how easy it would have been for a girl of fourteen to "go bad." I had no real supervision after that fateful day in July 1942; I could have done anything I pleased with no one to answer to. But my parents' influence, short-lived as it was, had such a powerful impact on me that the idea of straying from the straight and narrow was unthinkable. I am relieved when I think that at least I have nothing shameful to hide, no dark corners, no skeletons. I never hurt anyone intentionally, and I fought back only when I was attacked.

Nevertheless, the scars are there; they keep me in touch with my weaknesses and my faults, cause me to be introspective. Now, I like much of what I see inside.

"Take care of Josette." That was a tall order to a girl of fourteen, but my love and my admiration for my parents was so great that I couldn't disappoint them. Josette was a gift from them to me, my only heritage. Every time I was impatient or unkind to her (and I have been many times), a drop of guilt entered my soul. Before long the drops accumulated until they formed a puddle. It was then—before I allowed myself to drown in guilt—that I contemplated writing this book, so that I could understand more clearly the events in my life.

I have written for the many people who, like Josette and me, have been denied the love, the affection, and, most of all, the guidance of parents. Some of us are still scared and misunderstood. Some of us keep our memories bottled up in a corner of our minds, but feel a tremor each time we see a swastika or a Star of David or hear a disparaging remark about Jews. We keep silent because no one would understand that our wounds are not completely healed. There were children like Josette and me all over the world. Some were less fortunate: we at least had each other, and still do. But every day there are more of us. I do not know the answer; I pray someone will find it some day. I hope that the solution to this problem will not be preccipitated by another Holocaust.

Josette has been hurt more than I. I have fourteen years of fond memories of my parents. All Josette had was me. To this day Josette and I are very close, and I know we always will be.

In Epinal, in the huge Cimetière Saint-Michel there is a small enclosed area called, simply, the Jewish cemetery.

In this area an enormous monument in the shape of a large coffin stands on a pedestal. Around its perimeter are inscribed the names of Epinal's Jewish sons and daughters who were massacred in concentration camps. Among them are Papa's and Maman's names.

I first saw their names, carved in the stone, just a few years ago. When we left the cemetery, I told my husband and daughter, "I have finally come to my parents' funeral."

AFTERWORD

Papa Auguste and Guiguite died in 1946, Guiguite of a throat tumor on the day before her wedding. She was buried in her wedding gown—made from the material she'd asked me to send from the States. I continued to correspond with Maman Marie until she passed away seven years ago.

The senior Thiriets are no longer living. I corresponded with Mrs. Thiriet until she died. I believe that Raymond and Jacqueline are alive.

My cousin Michel Rosemberg died recently in tragic circumstances. He once confided to one of his sisters that he died emotionally the day his father died in the concentration camp. I have visited the other Rosemberg children on my various trips to France. Mrs. Rosemberg, who lived in a home for the aged, a beautiful converted castle near Paris, where Josette and I visited with her in the summer of 1980, died in April of this year.

Tante Brigitte, who is very old now, lives in Nancy. When I visited her last summer for the first time in twenty-five years, all my animosity vanished at the sight of this old lady who looked so much as I imagine Maman would now look.

My cousins Ida and Jeannine and their families live in Nancy.

Mr. Maurice and his family never returned from the concentration camp.

Of the Lassalas family, only dear Jeanne, Ririe, and her husband and their three children remain. Baptiste died of cancer many years ago, followed by La Mémé a few years later. Jeanne and I write to each other—as we have for the last thirty-seven years.

Tante Cecile and Uncle Albert are well. They, their daughter Jeannine, and her children all live in New York.

Tante Regine and Uncle Benno reside in Palm Beach, Florida, but still maintain a summer residence in New York.

To all the other kind people whose paths we crossed here and abroad, I give thanks. Although I do not recall their names, their contributions helped keep us alive, and we will always be grateful to them.

Last, Josette and I want to thank the United States for allowing us to become its citizens. It is a very special country that makes foreigners feel at home so quickly— and that gives to two orphans the freedom and opportunity to find, at last, a better life.

As Jacqueline Glicenstein's paren
were led away by the Gestapo, th
bade their fourteen-year-old daug
ter, "Take care of Josette," her fou
year-old sister. The place was Occ
pied France; the year, 1942.

Until the Nazis invaded Franc
the Glicensteins led a very comfo
able upper middle-class life in a tow
near Paris. For Jacqueline, a stude
in an exclusive private school, the d
ruption was especially bewilderin
born to parents who were not strict
religious, she thought of herself
French rather than Jewish. H
subsequent courageous struggle
obey her parents and survive in
brutal world is therefore all the mo
remarkable. As she moved from hi
ing place to hiding place, working as
maid to feed Josette and hersel
Jacqueline learned to accept narro
escapes as daily routine. Along th
way she found sympathy and gene
ous assistance — as well as betray
and cruel deprivation.